Interactive
Whiteboards

30 Activities to Engage All Learners

Made Easy

Getting Started

Comprehension

Aa Bb Vocabulary
Development

Prior

Graphic Organizers

Review

Author

Stephanie Paris

SHELL EDUCATION

Publishing Credits

Dona Herweck Rice, *Editor-in-Chief*; Lee Aucoin, *Creative Director*; Don Tran, *Print Production Manager*; Timothy J. Bradley, *Illustration Manager*; Sara Johnson, *Senior Editor*; Hillary Wolfe, *Editor*; James Anderson, *Associate Editor*; Robin Erickson, *Cover Designer/Interior Layout Designer*; Stephanie Reid, *Cover Photographer*; Corinne Burton, M.A. Ed., *Publisher*

Shell Education

5301 Oceanus Drive
Huntington Beach, CA 92649-1030
http://www.shelleducation.com

ISBN 978-1-4258-0685-9

©2011 Shell Educational Publishing, Inc.

WTP 3791

Table of Contents

Research and Introduction

Teachers and Students in the 21st Century

If you are a teacher right now, chances are that you remember having basal readers in elementary school, then, in middle and high school, lugging around English, mathematics, science, and history textbooks. Today's students might characterize the way you learned as "so last century"—and they would be right. Today's students are living and learning in the 21st century, and the way things used to be done is "history."

Gone are the days when students were individual, passive learners of facts and formulas. The students of today are collaborative, active learners who need to know where and how to get information from more than just memorizing and storing details from a single source, such as a textbook (Magaña and Frenkel 2009).

The teacher's role has transformed as well. Rather than being *disseminators*, modern teachers need to be *facilitators*. Students today are using the latest technology outside of school to entertain themselves, connect with friends, and instantly find information about anything that interests them. It only makes sense to use these tools in their classrooms, as well—under the guidance of a skilled teacher. In reality, few teachers have implemented the use of Web 2.0 applications, tools, podcasts, blogs, or wikis in their classrooms—perhaps because learning and using these technological tools seem daunting to those teachers who have not used these materials themselves. Yet educators who intend to continue teaching in the 21st century must begin to take steps toward technological literacy. One step that is effective and not too far beyond even a reluctant teacher's comfort zone is the use of interactive whiteboards as a teaching and learning tool.

Why Use Interactive Whiteboards?

In an article published in the November 2009 issue of *Educational Leadership*, Robert Marzano offers this conclusion based on research (Becker and Lee) regarding the use of interactive whiteboards in the classroom:

> "The study results indicated that, in general, using interactive whiteboards was associated with a 16 percentile point gain in student achievement. This means that we can expect a student at the 50th percentile in a classroom without the technology to increase to the 66th percentile in a classroom using whiteboards."

Marzano also predicts that the use of interactive whiteboards will "grow exponentially" and that "books like The Interactive Whiteboard Revolution (Becker and Lee 2009) attest to the depth and breadth of change this tool can promote in classroom practice."

How Are Interactive Whiteboards Different from Regular Whiteboards?

In the last 20 years, chalkboards were replaced with whiteboards. The only difference was material; the method of delivery was the same. The teacher wrote on the board any information that was used in the lesson, and then it was erased. In this century, interactive whiteboards are replacing traditional whiteboards, and the difference is radical in both material and delivery. An interactive whiteboard is a large display that is connected to a computer. The computer's screen is projected onto the display board where information is not only seen by the whole group, but can also be manipulated in real time. Lessons can include elements that could have never been shown on a traditional chalkboard or whiteboard, and anything displayed, changed, or written on an interactive whiteboard can be saved.

How Interactive Whiteboards Benefit Students

The 21st century classroom does have something in common with the classrooms of the past—that is, a diversity of students. In any given class, there may be high-achieving, average, low-performing, and struggling students. There may be students with low motivation to learn or high motivation to learn. There may be students whose first language is something other than English and students with special needs. Within these various groups will be students who have different learning modalities—visual, auditory, and tactile. Using interactive whiteboards can benefit all of these students (Beeland Jr. 2002; Torff and Tirotta 2010).

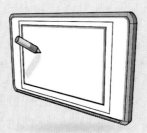

Interactive whiteboards...

- improve student participation
- increase motivation and engagement
- allow all students access to material and the ability to interact with it
- appeal to students at all levels of achievement
- help students focus and attend to lessons
- encourage student input and increase involvement
- provide opportunities for visual, auditory, and tactile experiences
- promote collaborative learning
- enhance exposure to various models of information and a variety of media
- give immediate feedback
- foster a sense of community in the classroom
- extend students' ability to access people and information outside the classroom
- afford the ability to save, print, and share lessons and notes

Teaching with Interactive Whiteboards— When More Is Less

Teaching and learning in recent years has been defined by standards, accountability, testing, and "leaving no child behind." The 21st century brings with it new challenges for teachers. Perhaps in the recent explosion of technology, you may feel as if it is you that is being left behind. First, if you are not a "techie," do not be discouraged. You can bring technology into your classroom one step at a time. Fortunately, using interactive whiteboards is a great way to do this. Do not fall into the trap of thinking that this is something more to add on top of your already-full workload. An interactive whiteboard is a tool that, in fact, does add more to your classroom by opening up a whole world of information, and can also mean less work for you. How? Consider these "more is less" time-saving features of using interactive whiteboards:

- If you are like most teachers, you have wasted time looking for lesson plans or notes you made for a previous lesson but finally ended up just redoing it. You probably have also wished that you had saved a lesson plan that worked particularly well, but it was lost once the lesson was over. Anything you do on an interactive whiteboard—from a prepared lesson and notes made right on the screen, to student-added input—can be saved, printed, and shared. A lesson on nouns that includes animated video and sound will be there next year when you want to teach the lesson again. Even if you are adept at saving your lesson plans and notes for future reference, interactive whiteboard lessons can capture the whole lesson, including any multimedia components such as pictures, sound, and animation and are all ready to use again whenever you want.

- How much time do you think you have spent writing out notes on the board or charts, making student worksheets, study sheets, or handouts, or preparing homework assignments and providing makeup work for students who have missed class? Interactive whiteboards save what you have prepared and can provide the exact lesson to any student who missed class or just needs a review. You can print out any or all parts of a lesson (without taking the time and resources to make photocopies), or they can be shared electronically.

- Perhaps the greatest time-saver created by interactive whiteboard lessons is in removing the constraints of independent lesson preparation. You can share interactive whiteboard lessons with colleagues—not just with teachers in your school, but around the country or even the world. Why reinvent the wheel when you can connect with other teachers who have been there, done that?

If interactive whiteboards are new to you, this book is a great place to start. You will find ready-made, easy-to-implement lessons across the curriculum. There are six sections with five activities per section, one in each of these five content areas: mathematics, science, social studies, reading, and writing. Once you have tried these lessons and seen for yourself how engaged and responsive your students can be, you will be "sold" on using this technology in the classroom.

Getting the Most from Interactive Whiteboards

Think of the interactive whiteboard as a tool with many versatile functions. At its most basic level, it can function as an electronic projector. However, limiting its use to this function would be like hiring a symphony and then asking only one musician to play! To get the most out of this technology and its multiple capabilities, you may want to explore Web-based resources. Although interactive whiteboards are relatively new, there are already many sites that have been created for teachers who want to use this technology in their classrooms. These sites range from sponsored sites to teacher networks. There is a large amount of supportive material—much of it free—including quite a bit of software. It is easy to find almost anything you might want to use in your classroom. Although much of the resource materials are classroom-quality, you will, of course, want to scrutinize each source before using any with students. There are even sites to help you weed through the vast resources available online. A good place to find guidance is your state's education website, which may direct you to any number of pre-screened and recommended resources. You can also join a teacher network where you can share information, reviews, and lessons with other teachers. Of course, many Shell Education products include interactive whiteboard compatible materials, as well!

These activities are helpful as you build your confidence and skill using the interactive whiteboard over time, but what if you just need something on the fly—maybe before or even during a lesson? How do you find something appropriate without wading through dozens of Web entries? The key is to enter specific search words in your preferred search engine and then scan the promising entries that appear and evaluate the sources. This can be done quickly, as seen in the following example:

During Mr. Haas' science lesson about the human body, a student asks how the heart pumps blood. In a matter of seconds, Mr. Haas can find several resources online that illustrate this, choose an appropriate one, download it, and display it. First, Mr. Haas types the key words *heart pumping* into the search bar engine of his Web browser. Several links are listed. He skims through them. Of the first five links, he sees two that may be appropriate for his demonstration. The other links have to do with transplants and heart pumps. Of the two links that claim to be animated videos of a pumping heart, Mr. Haas glances at the sources. One is **http://yourdoctor.com** and the other is **http://health.nih.gov/** and, although either link may be appropriate, Mr. Haas chooses the National Institutes of Health site to be certain. When he opens the site, he is pleased to see exactly what he needs. He can then project the video on the interactive whiteboard for all students to watch.

Getting the Most from Interactive Whiteboards *(cont.)*

If you have ever done a search on your Web browser, you know that finding what you want is not always that easy. Keep in mind that you greatly improve your chances of quickly locating quality resources by entering specific, narrow search terms and then examining the sources of the results. Many sources are easily questionable—they may or may not be accurate or appropriate. Others, such as government agencies, libraries, universities, museums, and reputable organizations or foundations, are better bets. Although, if you cannot identify a source from its abbreviation in a listing, look for the suffixes *.gov* (government) or *.edu* (education) in Web addresses. If the topic appears to be what you need, but you are unsure of its origin, you can always open it to check the content and the source. ***Note:*** As a teacher, always be concerned about the quality and the appropriateness of any content students might see or access over the Internet. Teaching students how to screen searches is a very valuable and necessary part of using computers in the classroom. In the example of Mr. Haas, he could have used his search as a model and walked the students through his screening process.

Here are more tips about Internet resources:

- If you are looking for a fun activity, add the words *game*, *fun*, or *puzzle* to the search term, such as "multiplication fact *fun*" or "state capital *puzzle*."
- If you are looking for an illustration, specify *photo*, *drawing*, *graph*, or *painting* in your search options.

Finally, keep in mind that, while you can easily download images, sounds, video, articles, and a host of other things, you and your students are required to abide by copyright and fair use laws and restrictions. Again, teachers can model this by demonstrating where and how to find copyright information on websites and postings. Impress upon students that they must be responsible, good-members-in-standing of the digital community.

Organization and Management

Adapting to Interactive Whiteboards

As a teacher, you are already skilled in organization and management. Adapting to using online resources and interactive whiteboards should be just a matter of shifting from the "paper" world to the "digital" world. In many ways, organization of digital files is easier (and certainly more compact) than handling physical stacks of books, lessons, resources, and records. Generally, you will want to save files and organize them in folders in much the same way you do on your home computer. However, there are a few tips to follow and pitfalls to avoid.

- **Do not put any personal information or files on the computer you use at school.** If possible, make this a dedicated computer on which only school lessons and other non-sensitive files are kept. Even if you do not share your school computer or intend to share files with colleagues, treat the computer as if anything on it could be seen by anyone without any cause for concern. This includes any identifying information about yourself or your students, such as last names or email addresses.

- **Be meticulous about naming your files.** Although you may have files on your personal computer labeled "Joe's Vacation Pictures," you will want to be very precise and specific when naming your files for school use. If possible, include tags that could be picked up as keywords in a search. For example, a file named "LStundras" may have seemed perfectly clear when you taught tundras in Life Science, but even if you do remember the name, it is not very "searchable." A better choice would be "Life Science Gr. 7 tundra IWB lesson with photos." Then, if you or another teacher with whom you are collaborating look for any of these key words (e.g., *tundra, life science, IWB lesson, Gr. 7, photos of tundra, science Gr. 7, Gr. 7 tundra,* and so on) your lesson will be the immediate result of that search.

- **Avoid saving too many files.** A common pitfall when working with files is to save several versions of the same file. You may want to do this while you are working on a project, but once it is done, delete the older versions. If you do want to save different versions of a lesson, for example, the same lesson differentiated for an advanced group and an ELL class, be sure to label each one clearly.

Teacher Versus Machine— How to Win

Teachers are responsible for managing all operations. Using the interactive whiteboard is clearly more complex than using a piece of chalk or a dry-erase marker. First, you will notice that instead of having to have your back to the class as you write on the board or chart, you can now face the group (and monitor their behavior, attentiveness, reactions, and responses). You will still need to manage the equipment, but you will no longer need to have "eyes in the back of your head." If you fear that technology may defeat you by not doing what you want or expect, take heart. In the struggle of teacher versus machine, you can take steps to ensure that you win.

1. Leave lots of space around the whiteboard—in front and to the sides—to allow access without blocking the beam.

2. Make sure that the whiteboard is mounted high enough for everyone to see but low enough for students to touch. (For young students, provide a stool or a long-handled pointer. Some students benefit by using a tennis ball instead of their fingers.)

3. Place the computer or keyboard near the whiteboard so that text can be added without constantly having to move across the classroom to access input.

4. Check the sound level and quality of the speaker. If it is insufficient for your needs, add external speakers.

5. Use electrical tape to secure the cord to avoid tripping.

6. If the equipment is on a cart, place it in an area where it is not likely to get bumped or jarred.

7. Set the screen resolution to 1024 x 768, and choose fonts and sizes that can easily be seen from the farthest point in the room. Avoid white or pale colors as backgrounds. To reduce glare from windows, improve the contrast of the material on the screen by using dark backgrounds with white or light-colored text and graphics.

8. Whenever possible, create documents that fit "as is" on the screen. In other words, add page breaks to avoid having to scroll up and down. Include an end-of-page marker, and keep tools at the top of the page. Use full-screen or presentation mode to show the entire page.

9. In any application, make use of the "floating" tools provided, such as highlighters and colored pens.

10. When projecting a website, use the full-screen function.
Tip: In Internet Explorer, press F11 to remove all toolbars from view. In *Safari*, click **Command**+**Shift**+\. Doing this will eliminate unnecessary distractions and allow the page to display larger.

What Can You Do With an Interactive Whiteboard?

The lessons and activities in this book are good starting points for implementing the use of interactive whiteboards in the classroom. As you become more comfortable using this technology, you may want to save a duplicate copy and adapt the activities to place your own content and ideas into them. In addition to these activities, there are other things that you can do with interactive whiteboards. With an interactive whiteboard, anything you can create or view on a computer can be displayed, manipulated, saved, shared, or printed. The possibilities are endless. Here are just a few ideas for using interactive whiteboards with large or small groups:

• **PowerPoint® presentations** These can be teacher-made or student-created projects.	• **Group analysis and critical thinking** Project a piece of literature to discuss, student-written stories to read and share, or a reader's theater script to perform.
• **Interactive worksheets** Use these for guided practice, demonstration, or review.	• **Primary sources** Share original documents, music, art, and so on. (Check copyrights for intended use beyond viewing.) Play videos of interviews, news clips, documentaries, and so on.
• **Graphic organizers** In addition to the ones provided in this book, you can tap into dozens more that are topic specific or open-ended. You can also create and save your own.	• **Interactive multimedia** Make any presentation interactive and multimedia by adding pictures, sounds, commentaries, highlighting, captions, and notes.
• **Previewing and practice** Preview a lesson by displaying a picture or excerpt and hear students' responses to determine prior knowledge. Display practice tests to work on together or demonstrate how to complete test items or directions.	• **Publish and share student work** Encourage students to share the products of their efforts: stories and other written pieces, projects, research results, original artwork, and so on.
• **Prewriting activities** Project brainstorming sessions, note-taking ideas, sentence starters, grammar rules, pictures to stimulate discussions or to prompt writing, and so on.	• **Post class information** Display notices, calendars, schedules, homework assignments, and more.

How to Use This Book

The *Interactive Whiteboards Made Easy* series was created to provide teachers with model activities for integrating interactive whiteboard technology into their instruction. The activities are meant to show how easily interactive whiteboards can be used across the content areas of mathematics, science, social studies, reading, and writing to enhance instruction and complement lessons that are already in place within the core curriculum. The information on pages 12–15 outlines the major components and purposes for each activity.

Activity Plan

The standard provided here includes the content-area objective of the activity.

The tab describes the activity section: Getting Started Activities, Vocabulary Development Activities, Activating Prior Knowledge Activities, Graphic Organizer Activities, Comprehension Activities, and Review Activities.

The interactive whiteboard skills used in the activity are outlined here. Review those skills using the How-to Guide found on pages 118–123.

The file name, title, and page number of the student activity sheet, as well as any additional materials necessary to complete the activity are listed here.

The procedures for the activity are listed here. The interactive whiteboard skills are boldfaced throughout the procedures to call attention to when they are used.

Standard: Uses phonetic and structural analysis techniques, syntactic structure, and semantic context to decode unknown words

Getting Started Activities

Anagram Words

Materials
- Level 6 Interactive Whiteboard File (level6.notebook)
- *Word Mix-up* activity sheet (p. 22)

Interactive Whiteboard Skills
- Advancing pages
- Dragging objects or text
- Using the screen shade

Procedure
1. Launch the Level 6 Notebook file by double-clicking on the icon from the Teacher Resource CD. Press the arrow next to Getting Started activities. Begin this activity by pressing on the Anagram Words title from the list.

2. Tell the class they are going to work on anagrams. Anagrams are words that can be unscrambled to make a new word.

3. Press the arrow to **advance** to the first activity page on the interactive whiteboard. Distribute copies of the *Word Mix-up* activity sheet (p. 22). Have students cut out the letters at the bottom of the page. Students can work with partners or in small groups. Invite students up to the board to press the yellow star to reveal the relating factor (*Healthy Foods*).

4. Slide the shade screen to the right to reveal the first anagram (*beagle vest*). Have students gather letters in front of them.

5. Have students write these words in the first box on their activity sheets

6. Instruct students to move the letters around until they have created two new words. Remind them that they must use all the letters in *beagle vest* to create the new word. If some students are struggling to create the anagram, give the students a clue by **dragging** the first letter of the anagram to the empty white box below. In the first anagram, **drag** the letter *v*.

7. After students have figured out the first anagram, invite someone up to the board to **drag** the letters and create the correct word in the white box below.

8. Use the magnifying glass that is at the bottom of the page to reveal the correct answer (*vegetables*) by moving it over the space beneath the first box. This allows students to check their work. If they solved the word incorrectly, have students put a line through their incorrect response and write the correct word below it.

9. Slide the **screen shade** to the right to reveal the second anagram (*turf is*). Repeat steps 5–8 with the second word. If students need a clue about this word, **drag** the letter *f* to the box below the anagram (*fruits*).

20   #50685—*Interactive Whiteboards Made Easy: Level 6*   © Shell Education

---

Activity Plan *(cont.)*

The icon represents the section in which this activity belongs. It corresponds to the information found on the tab on the edge of the page.

Additional lesson ideas are included to link the activity to content-area instruction.

A sample of the interactive whiteboard files for each activity are shown here to help teachers visualize how the activity is conducted before practicing with the actual file.

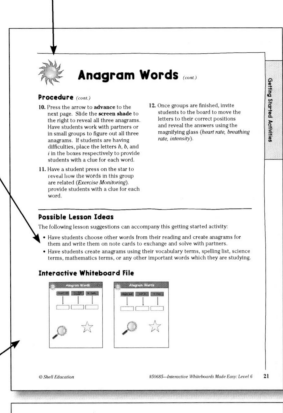

The student activity sheet mirrors the interactive whiteboard pages, allowing all students to participate in the activity, even if they are not at the board. The activity sheet can also be used for formative assessment.

Teacher Resource CD

The Teacher Resource CD provided with this book contains electronic copies of all of the student reproducible activity sheets. It also contains the interactive whiteboard files that are used with each activity. In addition, teacher-planning resources are included. (See page 127 for detailed information on the CD.)

Here are some general system requirements: For Mac®, Power PC® G3 500 MHz or faster processor, or Intel® 1.33 GHz or faster processor, 128 MB of RAM. For PC, Windows® Intel® Pentium® II 450 GHz or faster processor, 128 MB of RAM.

Integrating This Resource into Your Curriculum

When planning instruction using this resource, it is important to look ahead at your instructional time line and daily lesson plans to see where the activities provided in *Interactive Whiteboards Made Easy* can best be integrated. The Content-Area Matrix (p. 117) and the Standards Correlation (pp. 16–17) are two resources that can help you choose which activities will best fit your planned curriculum. Preview the activities to find one that correlates with the objective listed in your time line. The *Instructional Time Line* template (p. 15) is provided to help integrate this resource into long-range planning.

Implementing the Activities

After integrating this resource into your instructional time line, use the steps below to help you implement the activities.

1. Familiarize yourself with the written activity. Use the thumbnail image of the interactive whiteboard pages to visualize how the steps may take place while conducting the activity.

2. Review the Interactive Whiteboard Skills section of the lesson. Make sure you are comfortable with all of the skills necessary to conduct the lesson. If review is needed, look at the How-to Guide (pp. 118–123) sections that correspond with those required skills.

3. Open the interactive whiteboard file that accompanies the activity. Practice the activity to make sure you are comfortable with the necessary interactive whiteboard skills and how to use the pages to enhance your instruction.

4. If desired, invite a colleague to watch you practice delivering instruction of some or all of the activity. The technology becomes easier to use the more often you practice!

Instructional Time Line

Directions: In the first column, record the date of the lesson. In the second column, record the standards and/or objectives to be taught with that lesson. In the third column, write a brief description of the lesson to be taught. In the fourth and fifth columns, write the *Interactive Whiteboards Made Easy* activities and page numbers to be used to support the lesson. In the sixth column, include any adaptations or notes regarding the activities and/or lessons.

Instructional Time Line					
Date	Standard/ Objective	Lesson Description	Interactive Whiteboards Made Easy Activity	Pages	Adaptations or Notes

Standards Correlation

Shell Education is committed to producing educational materials that are research and standards based. In this effort, we have correlated all of our products to the academic standards of all 50 states, the District of Columbia, and the Department of Defense Dependent Schools.

How to Find Standards Correlations

To print a customized correlation report of this product for your state, visit our website at **http://www.shelleducation. com** and follow the on-screen directions. If you require assistance in printing correlation reports, please contact Customer Service at 1-877-777-3450.

Purpose and Intent of Standards

The No Child Left Behind legislation mandates that all states adopt academic standards that identify the skills students will learn in kindergarten through grade twelve. While many states had already adopted academic standards prior to NCLB, the legislation set requirements to ensure the standards were detailed and comprehensive.

Standards are designed to focus instruction and guide adoption of curricula. Standards are statements that describe the criteria necessary for students to meet specific academic goals. They define the knowledge, skills, and content students should acquire at each level. Standards are also used to develop standardized tests to evaluate students' academic progress.

Teachers are required to demonstrate how their lessons meet state standards. State standards are used in development of all of our products, so educators can be assured they meet the academic requirements of each state.

McREL Compendium

We use the Mid-continent Research for Education and Learning (McREL) Compendium to create standards correlations. Each year, McREL analyzes state standards and revises the compendium. By following this procedure, McREL is able to produce a general compilation of national standards. Each lesson in this product is based on one or more McREL standards. The chart on the following page lists each standard taught in this product and the page numbers for the corresponding lessons.

TESOL Standards

The lessons in this book promote English language development for English language learners. The standards listed on page 18 support the language objectives presented throughout the lessons.

Lesson Title	Content Area	Standard
Anagram Words (pp. 20–22)	Reading	Uses phonetic and structural analysis techniques, syntactic structure, and semantic context to decode unknown words
Analogies (pp. 23–25)	Science	Understands atmospheric processes and the water cycle
Calendar (pp. 26–28)	Writing	Writes in order to communicate ideas and inform
Daily Geography (pp. 29–31)	Social Studies	Understands the characteristics and uses of maps, globes, and other geographical tools and technologies

Lesson Title	Content Area	Standard
Daily Mathematics (pp. 32–34)	Mathematics	Uses a variety of strategies in the problem solving process
Alike and Different (pp. 35–37)	Science	Knows that Earth is comprised of layers including a core, mantle, lithosphere, hydrosphere and atmosphere
Concept of Definition Map (pp. 38–40)	Reading	Uses a variety of strategies to extend reading vocabulary
Example/Nonexample (pp. (41–43)	Mathematics	Understands and applies basic and advanced concepts of the properties of numbers
Total Physical Response (pp. 44–46)	Social Studies	Understands significant characteristics of early Chinese society and religion
Word Tiles (pp. 47–49)	Writing	Uses grammatical and mechanical conventions in written compositions
Analyze the Picture (pp. 50–52)	Social Studies	Understands the major developments and chronology of the Revolutionary War and the roles of its political, military, and diplomatic leaders
Anticipation Guide (pp. 53–55)	Reading	Establishes and adjusts purposes for reading
Historical Document (pp. 56–58)	Writing	Writes in response to literature
List, Group, Label (pp. 59–61)	Science	Knows ways in which living things can be classified
Picture Predictions (pp. 62–64)	Mathematics	Understands rotations and dilations
Venn Diagram (pp. 65–67)	Social Studies	Understands the processes that contributed to the emergence of agricultural societies around the world
Flow Chart (pp. 68–70)	Mathematics	Understands the correct order of operations for performing arithmetic computations
KWL Chart (pp. 71–73)	Writing	Gathers and uses information for research purposes
T-Chart (pp. 74–76)	Reading	Knows the parts of speech and their functions
Web Map (pp. 77–79)	Science	Knows ways in which living things can be classified
Cause and Effect (pp. 80–82)	Science	Understands Earth's composition and structure
Classify and Categorize (pp. 83–85)	Mathematics	Understands and applies basic and advanced properties of the concepts of geometry
Main Idea and Details (pp. 86–88)	Social Studies	Understands the role of art in conveying ideas in China and Japan (e.g., how nature is portrayed in Chinese and Japanese brush paintings)
Sequencing (pp. 89–91)	Reading	Understands the use of specific literary devices (e.g., foreshadowing, flashback, progressive and digressive time, suspense)
Summarizing (pp. 92–94)	Writing	Writes in response to literature
Content Links (pp. 95–97)	Science	Understands the structure and properties of matter
Game Board (pp. 98–100)	Reading	Understands the use of language in literary works to convey mood, images, and meaning
Guess It! (pp. 101–103)	Social Studies	Understands the shifts and social framework of Roman society
Question It! (pp. 104–106)	Mathematics	Use a variety of strategies in the problem-solving process
Draw and Guess (pp. 107–109)	Writing	Uses grammatical and mechanical conventions in written compositions

TESOL Standards

Lesson	Content Area	Standard
All lessons	All content areas	To use English to communicate in social settings: Students will use English to participate in social interactions
All lessons	All content areas	To use English to communicate in social settings: Students will interact in, through, and with spoken and written English for personal expression and enjoyment
All lessons	All content areas	To use English to communicate in social settings: Students will use learning strategies to extend their communicative competence
All lessons	All content areas	To use English to achieve academically in all content areas: Students will use English to interact in the classroom
All lessons	All content areas	To use English to achieve academically in all content areas: Students will use English to obtain, process, construct, and provide subject matter information in spoken and written form
All lessons	All content areas	To use English to achieve academically in all content areas: Students will use appropriate learning strategies to construct and apply academic knowledge
All lessons	All content areas	To use English in socially and culturally appropriate ways: Students will use the appropriate language variety, register, and genre according to audience, purpose, and setting
All lessons	All content areas	To use English in socially and culturally appropriate ways: Students will use nonverbal communication appropriate to audience, purpose, and setting
All lessons	All content areas	To use English in socially and culturally appropriate ways: Students will use appropriate learning strategies to extend their sociolinguistic and sociocultural competence

Notes

Getting Started Activities

Anagram Words

Materials

- Level 6 Interactive Whiteboard File (level6.notebook)
- *Word Mix-up* activity sheet (p. 22)

Interactive Whiteboard Skills

- Advancing pages
- Dragging objects or text
- Using the screen shade

Procedure

1. Launch the Level 6 Notebook file by double-clicking on the icon from the Teacher Resource CD. Press the arrow next to Getting Started activities. Begin this activity by pressing on the Anagram Words title from the list.

2. Tell the class they are going to work on anagrams. Anagrams are words that can be unscrambled to make a new word.

3. Press the arrow to **advance** to the first activity page on the interactive whiteboard. Distribute copies of the *Word Mix-up* activity sheet (p. 22). Have students cut out the letters at the bottom of the page. Students can work with partners or in small groups. Invite students up to the board to press the yellow star to reveal the relating factor (*Healthy Foods*).

4. Slide the **screen shade** to the right to reveal the first anagram (*beagle vest*). Have students gather letters in front of them.

5. Have students write these words in the first box on their activity sheets.

6. Instruct students to move the letters around until they have created two new words. Remind them that they must use all the letters in *beagle vest* to create the new word. If some students are struggling to create the anagram, give the students a clue by **dragging** the first letter of the anagram to the empty white box below. In the first anagram, **drag** the letter *v*.

7. After students have figured out the first anagram, invite someone up to the board to **drag** the letters and create the correct word in the white box below.

8. Use the magnifying glass that is at the bottom of the page to reveal the correct answer (*vegetables*) by moving it over the space beneath the first box. This allows students to check their work. If they solved the word incorrectly, have students put a line through their incorrect response and write the correct word below it.

9. Slide the **screen shade** to the right to reveal the second anagram (*turf is*). Repeat steps 5–8 with the second word. If students need a clue about this word, **drag** the letter *f* to the box below the anagram (*fruits*).

Anagram Words *(cont.)*

Procedure *(cont.)*

10. Press the arrow to **advance** to the next page. Slide the **screen shade** to the right to reveal all three anagrams. Have students work with partners or in small groups to figure out all three anagrams. If students are having difficulties, place the letters *h*, *b*, and *i* in the boxes respectively to provide students with a clue for each word.

11. Have a student press on the star to reveal how the words in this group are related (*Exercise Monitoring*). Provide students with a clue for each word.

12. Once groups are finished, invite students to the board to move the letters to their correct positions and reveal the answers using the magnifying glass (*heart rate, breathing rate, intensity*).

Possible Lesson Ideas

The following lesson suggestions can accompany this getting started activity:

- Have students choose other words from their reading and create anagrams for them and write them on note cards to exchange and solve with partners.
- Have students create anagrams using their vocabulary terms, spelling list, science terms, mathematics terms, or any other important words which they are studying.

Interactive Whiteboard File

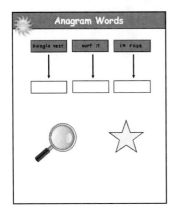 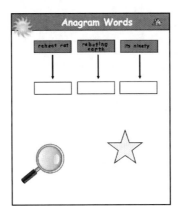

Name: _____

Word Mix-up

Directions: Cut out the letters below. Follow your teacher's directions to unscramble the words and write the relationship among the words.

⬇	⬇	⬇
_____	_____	_____

How are the words related? _____

⬇	⬇	⬇
_____	_____	_____

How are the words related? _____

a	a	a	a	a	a	b	b	e
e	e	e	e	e	e	e	f	g
g	g	h	h	i	i	i	i	i
l	n	n	n	n	r	r	r	r
r	r	s	s	s	s	t	t	t
t	t	t	t	t	u	v	y	

 #50685—Interactive Whiteboards Made Easy: Level 6

Analogies

Materials

- Level 6 Interactive Whiteboard File (level6.notebook)
- *Analogies Matter* activity sheet (p. 25)

Interactive Whiteboard Skills

- Advancing pages
- Dragging objects or text

Procedure

1. Launch the Grade 6 Notebook file by double-clicking on the icon from the Teacher Resource CD. Press the arrow next to Getting Started activities. Begin this activity by pressing on the Analogies title from the list.

2. Review what an analogy is with the class. Remind students that an analogy is a comparison between two different things in order to try and find some similarities between them.

3. Press the arrow to **advance** to the first activity page on the interactive whiteboard. Discuss the two words on the left side of the page (*atom* and *matter*). Invite students to try and think of ways these two words are related to one another.

4. Distribute a copy of the *Analogies Matter* activity sheet (p. 25) to each student. Have students fill in the first analogy frame with the words *atom* and *matter*. Now have students focus on the right side of the analogy frame and have them write the word *brick* in their frame.

5. Explain to students that there are three words from which to choose to finish the analogy frame (*clay*, *wall*, or *water*).

6. Once students have chosen and recorded answers on their activity sheets, invite a student up to the interactive whiteboard to tell which word he or she chose. Instruct the student to explain his or her reasoning. Then, have the student **drag** his or her selection to the empty white box to complete the analogy frame. If the student has chosen the correct selection, a checkmark will appear. If the student has chosen an incorrect selection, an X will appear.

7. As a class, say the whole analogy together: "*Atom is to matter as brick is to wall.*"

8. Press the arrow to **advance** to the next page. Repeat steps 4–6 for the next analogy (*corrosion is to rust as burning is to ash*).

9. Press the arrow to **advance** to the next page. For this page, the students will need to place all of the terms in the correct places to complete the analogy frame.

10. Have students work with partners to complete this part of the activity. As students complete their frames, have them discuss with their partners the relationships they have found between the terms.

Analogies *(cont.)*

Procedure *(cont.)*

11. Once all of the pairs have completed their frames, invite a pair of students up to the interactive whiteboard and have them **drag** the terms to fill out the frame. Instruct the pair to explain their reasoning and how the two pairs of terms are related (H_2O *is to water as NaCL is to table salt*).

12. Press the red star at the bottom of the page to reveal the correct answer to the analogy frame. As a class, say the whole analogy together: "*H_2O is to water as NaCL is to table salt.*"

13. Press the arrow to **advance** to the next page. Repeat steps 9–11 for the last analogy (*solid is to liquid as liquid is to gas*).

Possible Lesson Ideas

The following lesson suggestions can accompany this getting started activity:

- Have students build a model of a specific molecule using found objects brought from their homes.
- Have students create their own analogies about matter. Instruct them to write the analogies on four different flashcards and exchange them with other students to solve them.

Interactive Whiteboard File

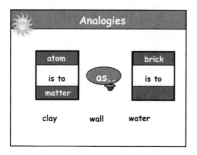
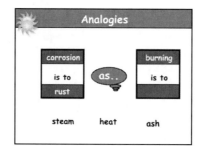
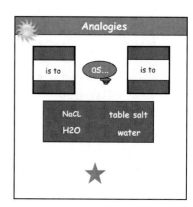

Analogies Matter

Directions: Follow your teacher's directions to complete the analogies using the boxes below.

1.

is to

as...

is to

2.

is to

as...

is to

3.

is to

as...

is to

4.

is to

as...

is to

Calendar

Materials

- Level 6 Interactive Whiteboard File (level6.notebook)
- *Today's Snapshot* activity sheet (p. 28)

Interactive Whiteboard Skills

- Advancing pages
- Dragging objects or text
- Using the pen tool

Procedure

1. Launch the Level 6 Notebook file by double-clicking on the icon from the Teacher Resource CD. Press the arrow next to Getting Started activities. Begin this activity by pressing on the Calendar title from the list. All of the components of this file have been infinitely cloned so that they can be used as frequently as needed.

2. Press the arrow to **advance** to the first activity page on the interactive whiteboard. Tell students that they are going to do some short activities to start the day.

3. Invite a student up to the interactive whiteboard and have the student **drag** the correct days into the white boxes across the top of the page.

4. Invite a new student up to the board to **drag** the current day, month, date, and year to the white box in the middle of the page.

5. Distribute copies of the *Today's Snapshot* activity sheet (p. 28) to students. Then have them write the correct date on the first line of their activity sheets and remind them to use correct punctuation.

6. Press the arrow to **advance** to the next page. This activity helps students organize their time and plan ahead. Invite a student up to the interactive whiteboard to use the **pen tool** to write the day's schedule and upcoming events on the calendar in the appropriate spaces. Include assemblies, homework, lunch schedule, or whatever information your class members need to get a clear idea of how they will need to use their time. Have students record the information for the day and important upcoming events on their activity sheets.

7. Press the arrow to **advance** to the next page. This activity helps students practice fact families. **Drag** three numbers into the white boxes. Use two-digit numbers, three-digit numbers, or decimals, if you like (e.g., *.4, .5, .2*). Invite a student up to the interactive whiteboard and use the **pen tool** to complete the fact family for those three numbers. Have the other students record the fact family and problems on their activity sheets.

Calendar *(cont.)*

Procedure *(cont.)*

8. Press the arrow to **advance** to the next page. This activity helps students practice their writing skills. You can either choose the quick-write topic in accordance with the day of the month (e.g., if it is the first Tuesday of the month, the students would write on the topic, *"Friends are important because…"*), or you can select a student to choose a topic at random. Either way, **drag** an X from the top of the page into the box of the topic selected. This will help you remember which topics have been covered and which are still available for use.

Possible Lesson Ideas

The following lesson suggestions can accompany this getting started activity:

- Have students create their own quick-write topics and write them on note cards. Shuffle the cards and allow students to pick them at random when it is time for a quick-write.
- Have students pick one of their quick write topics to expand into a full story or essay.
- Have students keep a learning journal to record the things that they learn on each day of school. Students record the date and the day of school (25th day, 100th day, etc.) before writing about what they learned.

Interactive Whiteboard File

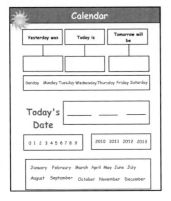

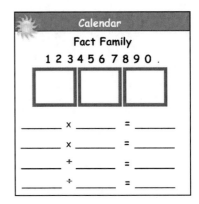

Name: _____

Today's Snapshot

Directions: Record details about the calendar activities today according to the directions from your teacher.

Today's date:

_____

Planning:

Monday	Tuesday	Wednesday	Thursday	Friday	Saturday	Sunday

Today's fact family:

_____ X _____ = _____   _____ ÷ _____ = _____

_____ X _____ = _____   _____ ÷ _____ = _____

My quick write:

_____

_____

_____

_____

_____

_____

_____

_____

_____

_____

_____

Daily Geography

Materials

- Level 6 Interactive Whiteboard File (level6.notebook)
- *Daily Geography* activity sheet (p. 31)

Interactive Whiteboard Skills

- Advancing pages
- Dragging objects or text
- Pinning pages
- Using dual page display

Procedure

1. Launch the Level 6 Notebook file by double-clicking on the icon from the Teacher Resource CD. Press the arrow next to Getting Started activities. Begin this activity by pressing on the Daily Geography title from the list.

2. Distribute copies of the *Daily Geography* activity sheet (p. 31) to students.

3. Press the arrow to **advance** to the first activity page on the interactive whiteboard. Allow students to share their observations.

4. Invite a student to the interactive whiteboard to **drag** the pull tab out from the side. Have the student read the question to the class (*Which city is the farthest north?*)

5. In box "1" on their activity sheets, instruct students to record their answer to the question. As a class, discuss the question and the answer (*Vergina*).

6. Repeat steps 4 and 5 for the remaining pull tabs (2: *Peloponnesos*; 3: *The Aegean Sea*; 4: *Sparta*).

7. Once students have completed those four questions, press the arrow to **advance** to the next page.

8. Give students time to look at the new map displayed on the screen. Allow students to share their observations with partners, and then with the class.

9. Tell students that they are going to be asked four questions about the map of Ancient Greece. In order for the students to be able to see the map and the questions at the same time, select the **dual page display**. Once selected, two pages will appear at the same time on the interactive whiteboard. In order for students to see the first question, press the arrow to **advance** to the next page.

Daily Geography *(cont.)*

Procedure *(cont.)*

10. The students will see two pages. The one on the left will be the map of Ancient Greece. The other page will have the first question students will need to answer. Read the questions aloud as a class. Tell students that these are multiple-choice questions, so they should record the letter of their choice in the corresponding boxes on their activity sheets.

11. Once all students have recorded their answers, invite a student to the interactive whiteboard and have him or her press the answer he or

she chose. If the chosen answer is correct, it will spin. If the chosen answer is not correct, nothing will happen.

12. To show question 2, select **view**, then **zoom**, then **pin page**. This will pin the page with the map of Ancient Greece. Press the arrow to **advance** to the next page to display question 2.

13. Repeat steps 10–12 to complete the remaining three questions about the ancient world.

Possible Lesson Ideas

The following lesson suggestions can accompany this getting started activity:

- Have students research a city from the ancient world and draw a map of that place. Have them include major points of interest such as temples, government buildings, and markets. If the exact layout of the city is not known, have students imagine how it might have looked.

- Have students research the architecture of one of the ancient cities. Have them design their dream homes as they would have appeared in that time and place.

- Have students design a trade route between two locations in the ancient world. Ask them to address how they would get their goods from place to place.

Interactive Whiteboard File

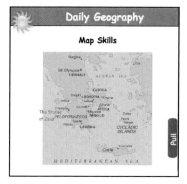
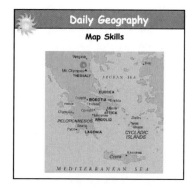
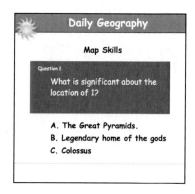

Daily Geography

Directions: Record information in the boxes below according to your teacher's directions.

1. Which city is the farthest north?	**2.** According to the map, on which island is the Statue of Zeus located?
3. Which sea separates Mt. Olympos from Troy?	**4.** Which is closer to Crete—Athens or Sparta?
5.	**6.**
7.	**8.**

Getting Started Activities

Daily Mathematics

Materials

- Level 6 Interactive Whiteboard File (level6.notebook)
- *Math Practice* activity sheet (p. 34)

Interactive Whiteboard Skills

- Advancing pages
- Dragging objects or text
- Using the spotlight tool

Procedure

1. Launch the Level 6 Notebook file by double-clicking on the icon from the Teacher Resource CD. Press the arrow next to Getting Started activities. Begin this activity by pressing on the Daily Mathematics title from the list.

2. Tell the class that they are going to do some math review problems. Distribute copies of the *Math Practice* activity sheet (p. 34) to students. Tell students that they are going to place their answers to the problems in the appropriate box on their activity sheets.

3. Divide the class into groups of four. Assign each student in the group a number between 1 and 4.

4. Tell students that they are going to play a game using the math problems on the screen. Press the arrow to **advance** to the first activity page on the interactive whiteboard and show them the problems that they will be solving. Tell students that they may work together to solve the problems, but must not show their answers until the appropriate time.

6. To reveal each problem for students to solve, use the **spotlight tool**. Once the **spotlight tool** is activated, you may change its shape. For this activity, the rectangle is most effective. ***Note:*** The **spotlight tool** may be added to the floating tool bar to make it easier for the teacher to access.

7. **Drag** the **spotlight tool** over the first problem you want the students to solve. Allow them to start solving the problem at the same time. Once each group and every student has an answer written down on their activity sheets, select a number between 1 and 4. Those students who were assigned the selected number must display their answers (e.g., if the number 2 was selected, only the students who are assigned number 2 will show their answers). If the student has the correct answer, his or her table will receive a point. ***Note:*** It is possible for multiple groups to receive points.

Daily Mathematics *(cont.)*

Procedure *(cont.)*

8. Continue **dragging** the **spotlight tool** until all of the problems have been completed. Present the winning team(s) with a reward, if desired.

Possible Lesson Ideas

The following lesson suggestions can accompany this getting started activity:

- Have students create their own math problems on flash cards. Instruct students to work with partners and exchange cards or have them flip one card over and the first student to solve the problem gets to keep the card.

- Place different math problems around the room and have students stand in front of a problem. Instruct students to solve their problems and record their answers. After one minute, have all the students rotate to a new problem and repeat the procedure. Continue until all of the problems are completed.

Interactive Whiteboard File

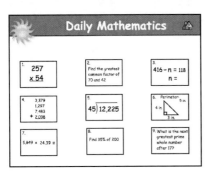

Name: _____

Math Practice

Directions: Record and solve each problem as it is displayed on the interactive whiteboard.

1.	2.	3.
4.	5.	6.
7.	8.	9.

 # Alike and Different

Materials

- Level 6 Interactive Whiteboard File (level6.notebook)
- *Drawing Comparisons* activity sheet (p. 37)

Interactive Whiteboard Skills

- Advancing pages
- Using dual page display
- Using the pen tool
- Using the text tool

Procedure

1. Launch the Level 6 Notebook file by double-clicking on the icon from the Teacher Resource CD. Press the arrow next to Vocabulary Development activities. Begin this activity by pressing on the Alike and Different title from the list.

2. Press the arrow to **advance** to the first activity page on the interactive whiteboard. Distribute copies of the *Drawing Comparisons* activity sheet (p. 37) to students. Tell students that they are going to be learning about some words that have to do with the layers of Earth.

3. Read aloud the word pairs in the Alike and Different map (*core* and *mantle*). Invite students who are familiar with the words to raise their hands.

4. Choose several students who are familiar with the words to share what they know about the words. Have students work either individually, in small groups, or as a whole class, to think about how the two words are alike.

5. Invite a student up to the interactive whiteboard to use the **pen tool** or the **text tool** to record ideas in the correct section of the chart. Have students also record this information on their activity sheets.

6. Now have the class think about and discuss how the words are different. Invite a student up to the interactive whiteboard to use the **pen tool** or the **text tool** to record ideas in the correct section of the chart. Instruct students to also record the information on their activity sheets.

7. Press the arrow to **advance** to the next page and bring up the next Alike and Different map. Complete steps 3–6 for the second pair of words (*lithosphere* and *crust*).

8. After the Alike and Different chart is completed, press the back arrow to **return** to the previous page. Then, use the **dual page display** to show both charts on the interactive whiteboard. Review both word pairs as a class and talk about how the pairs of words are both alike and different.

9. Repeat steps 7–8 for the third set of words (*hydrosphere* and *atmosphere*).

Vocabulary Development Activities

 # Alike and Different *(cont.)*

Possible Lesson Ideas

The following lesson suggestions can accompany this vocabulary development activity:

- Have students build models of Earth using different colors of modeling clay for each layer. Make a core out of a small ball of clay, then roll out layers and wrap them around. Cut the models in half with dental floss or a knife to reveal the strata.

- Do the Geology Cupcake Activity. Prepare cupcakes at home that have a variety (2–4) of colors swirled loosely together (you can use multiple flavors for this, as well). Include chocolate chips or other small candies in the batter and frost them lightly so that it is impossible to tell what is inside. Have students work in pairs or small groups. Issue each group one cupcake and a drinking straw. Have the students take "core samples" of their cupcakes using the straws. Then ask students to make predictions about what the inside might look like. After several core samples, have them draw their predictions. Then allow them to break open the cupcakes to see what the inside really looks like. Make sure you have enough extra cupcakes so that everyone can have a treat after the project!

Interactive Whiteboard File

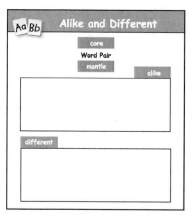  

 # Drawing Comparisons

Directions: Complete the charts below to compare the word pairs. Follow the directions from your teacher.

core
Word Pair
mantle

alike

different

lithosphere
Word Pair
crust

alike

different

hydrosphere
Word Pair
atmosphere

alike

different

Vocabulary Development Activities

Concept of Definition Map

Vocabulary Development Activities

Materials

- Level 6 Interactive Whiteboard File (level6.notebook)
- *Concept of Definition Map* activity sheet (p. 40)

Interactive Whiteboard Skills

- Advancing pages
- Using the pen tool
- Using the text tool

Procedure

1. Launch the Level 6 Notebook file by double-clicking on the icon from the Teacher Resource CD. Press the arrow next to Vocabulary Development activities. Begin this activity by pressing on the Concept of Definition Map title from the list.

2. Press the arrow to **advance** to the first activity page on the interactive whiteboard. Distribute three copies of the *Concept of Definition Map* activity sheet (p. 40) to each student.

3. Tell students that you are going to be discussing some words that they have probably heard, but that you will be trying to develop a more complete idea of what those words mean. Read aloud the vocabulary word in the middle of the concept map (*anthology*) and have students write the word on one of their activity sheets. Invite students who are familiar with the word to raise their hands.

4. Choose several students who are familiar with the word *anthology* to share what they think the word means. If necessary, share with students what the word means (*a collection of works such as poems, stories, or essays*).

5. As a class, decide on a definition that makes sense to everyone. Invite a student up to the interactive whiteboard to use the **pen tool** or the **text tool** to write that definition in the "What is it?" box. Instruct students to record that information on their activity sheets, as well.

6. As a class, discuss some things students know about the word *anthology*. Use this discussion to create a sentence about what the word is like.

7. Invite a student up to the interactive whiteboard to use the **pen tool** or the **text tool** to write the sentence in the "What is it like?" box. Instruct students to record that information on their own activity sheets.

8. Have students share examples of the word *anthology*. Students may share ideas such as *textbooks*, *collections of stories*, and *books of poetry*, or specific examples of anthologies.

Procedure *(cont.)*

9. Using the **pen tool**, invite students to draw the examples in the bottom three boxes of the concept map. Instruct students to draw those examples on their own activity sheets.

10. Press the arrow to **advance** to the next page.

11. Repeat steps 4–10 with the remaining words (*stanza: a number of lines forming a section within a poem; rhyme: having similar ending sounds between words*).

Possible Lesson Ideas

The following lesson suggestions can accompany this vocabulary development activity:

- Have students create concept of definition maps for one of their other vocabulary words and then present their maps to the class.
- Have students work with partners to compare and contrast different poems by one author or many authors.
- Divide students into groups. Have each group become an expert on a poem and produce a *Microsoft PowerPoint*® presentation to explain it.

Interactive Whiteboard File

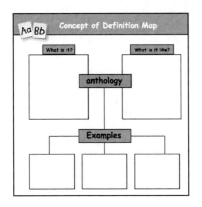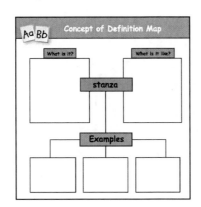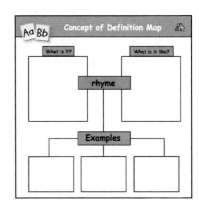

Vocabulary Development Activities

 # Concept of Definition Map

Directions: Complete the map according to the directions from your teacher.

What is it?　　　　　　　　　　　　**What is it like?**

Examples

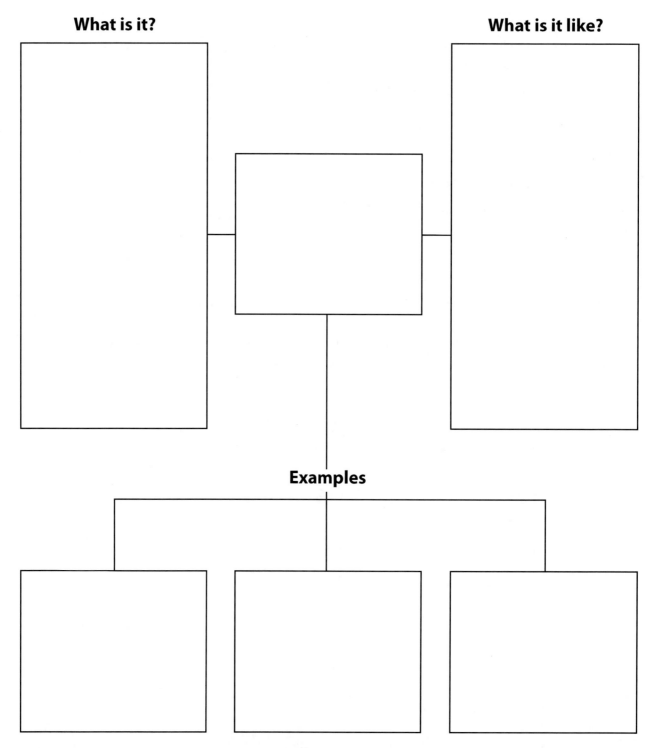

 # Example/Nonexample

Materials

- Level 6 Interactive Whiteboard File (level6.notebook)
- *Example/Nonexample* activity sheet (p. 43)

Interactive Whiteboard Skills

- Advancing pages
- Dragging objects or text
- Using the pen tool
- Using the text tool

Procedure

1. Launch the Level 6 Notebook file by double-clicking on the icon from the Teacher Resource CD. Press the arrow next to Vocabulary Development activities. Begin this activity by pressing on the Example/ Nonexample title from the list.

2. Press the arrow to **advance** to the first activity page on the interactive whiteboard.

3. Read aloud the term in the middle of the map (*whole number*). Invite students who have heard the term before to raise their hands.

4. Choose several students who are familiar with the term *whole number* to share some examples of whole numbers. Students can use words, phrases, numbers, pictures, or symbols to express their ideas. Allow them to come to the interactive whiteboard and use the **pen tool** or the **text tool** to write their ideas in the "Example" box.

5. Ask students to share additional ideas. Invite a student up to the interactive whiteboard to use the **pen tool** or the **text tool** to record the additional examples in the "Example" box.

6. Invite students to come up with ideas that are nonexamples of whole numbers. Allow them to come to the interactive whiteboard and use the **pen tool** or the **text tool** to write their ideas in the "Nonexample" box.

7. Distribute several copies of the *Example/Nonexample* activity sheet (p. 43) to students. Now turn students' attention to the numbers listed on the top of the page. Invite students up to the interactive whiteboard and have them **drag** the numbers to the appropriate boxes. Discuss how each number is either an example of a whole number or a nonexample of a whole number. When a student **drags** a number to a box he or she will receive instant feedback about his or her choice. Have students record the information on their activity sheets.

8. Press the arrow to **advance** to the next page. Repeat steps 3–8 for the word *integer*.

9. Press the arrow to **advance** to the next page.

Procedure (*cont.*)

10. Repeat steps 3–8 for the term *rational number* and have students record their work on their activity sheets.

11. As a class, discuss why certain numbers can be examples of some of the terms studied and nonexamples of other terms studied (e.g., *.14 is a rational number, but it is not an integer or a whole number*).

Possible Lesson Ideas

The following lesson suggestions can accompany this vocabulary development activity:

- Have students create and share mnemonics to help them remember the difference between whole numbers, rational numbers, and integers.

- Play "Integer War." Use a standard deck of cards and tell students that the red cards are negative and the black cards are positive. Have students deal the deck evenly among the players and then each person turns over his or her top card. Whoever has the highest card wins. [**Variation**: Have students turn over two cards and do an arithmetic problem (e.g., multiply the numbers) to determine who has the higher number.]

Interactive Whiteboard File

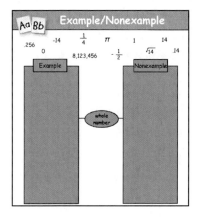
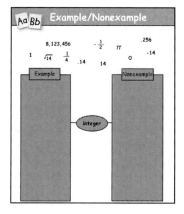
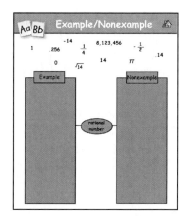

Vocabulary Development Activities

 # Example/Nonexample

Directions: Write the numbers from the number bank in the appropriate boxes below. Then add your own ideas.

Number Bank					
14	−14	1.4	$\frac{1}{4}$	$\sqrt{14}$	0
1	$-\frac{1}{2}$	.256	π	8,123,456	

Example

Nonexample

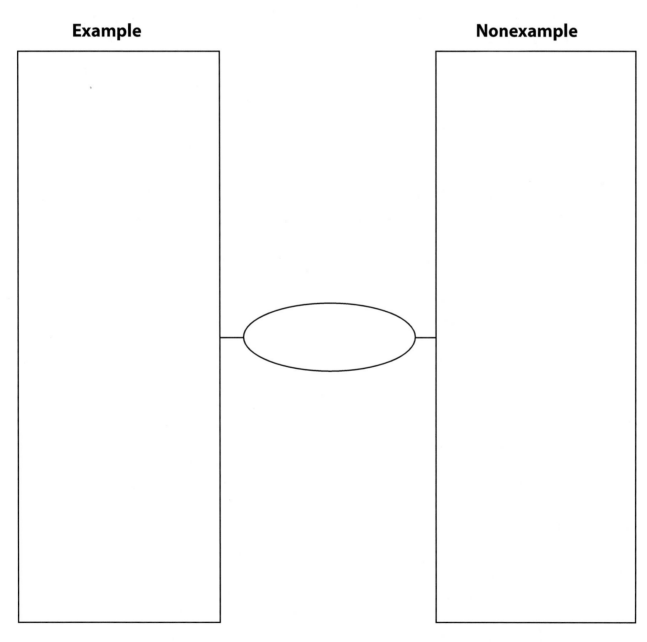

Total Physical Response

Vocabulary Development Activities

Materials

- Level 6 Interactive Whiteboard File (level6.notebook)
- *Dynasty Actions* activity sheet (p. 46)

Interactive Whiteboard Skills

- Advancing pages
- Using the cell shade
- Using the pen tool
- Using the text tool

Procedure

1. Launch the Level 6 Notebook file by double-clicking on the icon from the Teacher Resource CD. Press the arrow next to Vocabulary Development activities. Begin this activity by pressing on the Total Physical Response title from the list.

2. Press the arrow to **advance** to the first activity page on the interactive whiteboard. Distribute copies of the *Dynasty Actions* activity sheet (p. 46) to students.

3. Press the first **cell shade** located in the "Dynasty" column and read the term aloud to the students (*Xia Dynasty*). Tell students that you are going to use the chart and create movements to help them understand and remember the Chinese Dynasties you have been studying.

4. Choose students who are familiar with the term *Xia Dynasty* to share what they know about it. If a student knows characteristics of the dynasty or the time period, then select those two **cell shades** to reveal some key points. If you have further information that you would like to add as students learn more about the Xia, use the **text tool** to add it in by double-clicking on the cell.

5. Have students record that information on their activity sheets in the appropriate cells. Then reveal the appropriate **cell shade** to show the class an example of an important ruler who was a member of that dynasty.

6. Discuss the term for the Dynasty name. Ask volunteers to offer ideas for a physical action. Give several students an opportunity to share their ideas, and have the class decide which physical action they would like to use for the term *Xia Dynasty*.

7. Invite the student whose suggestion was chosen to the interactive whiteboard to use the **pen tool** or the **text tool** to write his or her initials in the box.

8. Press the next **cell shade** in the "Dynasty" column to reveal the second Dynasty name. Repeat steps 4–7 until the class has a physical response for all five of the Dynasty names and their activity sheets are completed.

9. Instruct students to stand and spread out around the room. Practice the motions by calling out each term, saying, "Show me _____" (e.g., "*Show me Xia Dynasty*").

 # Total Physical Response *(cont.)*

Procedure *(cont.)*

10. Allow students to repeat the term chorally as they make the physical response. As they become more familiar with the terms and physical responses, have students close their eyes before asking for a response. This is a great tool for formative assessment.

11. Press the arrow to **advance** to the next page. Invite a student up to the interactive whiteboard and press on the die. Have students individually, in small groups, or as a whole class make the physical response for the term that is displayed. Students should chorally say the word as they make the response.

12. Continue having students press the die until all of the terms have been displayed at least once.

Possible Lesson Ideas

The following lesson suggestions can accompany this vocabulary development activity:

- Have students create a map depicting the Silk Road and the goods that were traded in each major location.
- Have students create a Venn diagram comparing and contrasting the Legalist policies of the Qin government and the Confucian ideals of the Han.
- Have students each choose a technological, social, or artistic advancement that came from the Dynastic period of China. Have each student produce a *Microsoft PowerPoint*® presentation on his or her topic.

Interactive Whiteboard File

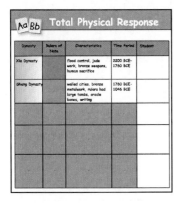 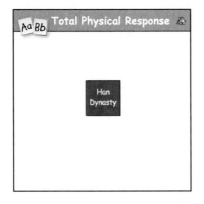

 # Dynasty Actions

Directions: Draw the actions chosen for each of the vocabulary words listed below.

Dynasty	Rulers of Note	Characteristics	Time Period	Action
Xia Dynasty				
Shang Dynasty				
Zhou Dynasty (Western and Eastern)				
Qin Dynasty				
Han Dynasty				

 # Word Tiles

Materials

- Level 6 Interactive Whiteboard File (level6.notebook)
- *When Is a Verb Not a Verb?* activity sheet (p. 49)

Procedure

1. Launch the Level 6 Notebook file by double-clicking on the icon from the Teacher Resource CD. Press the arrow next to Vocabulary Development activities. Begin this activity by pressing on the Word Tiles title from the list. ***Note:*** All of the word tiles are infinitely cloned so that students can see how root words can change based on their suffixes.

2. Press the arrow to **advance** to the first activity page on the interactive whiteboard. Distribute copies of the *When Is a Verb Not a Verb?* activity sheet (p. 49) to students.

3. Tell the class that they are going to focus on learning about verbals. A verb becomes a verbal when it is used as a different form of speech. Invite a student to read the first word box, *gerund.* Have a student volunteer **drag** the first pull tab to reveal some key points about gerunds. Make sure that the class knows that gerunds are formed when a verb ending in *-ing* is used as a noun.

4. To help students see how this works, **drag** a clone of the word tile verb *learn* from the bottom of the page. Then **drag** a clone of the word tile ending *-ing* from the top of the page, and place it next to the *learn* word tile.

Interactive Whiteboard Skills

- Advancing pages
- Dragging objects or text

Have the class brainstorm to think of sentences in which *learning* is used as a noun. (Possible example: *"Learning is very important!"*)

5. Have students record how a gerund is used (*as a noun*) on their activity sheets.

6. As a class, try making other words with the suffix *-ing* using the other word tiles. Have students add the new words to their activity sheets. (Possible words: *appearing, climbing, cooking, judging, playing, spelling, traveling, watching,* and *working.*) Point out that standard spelling rules apply, thus words with an *e* at the end must lose the *e* before adding the *-ing.*

7. Repeat steps 3–6 for the remaining types of verbals. (Possible words for infinitives: *to appear, to climb, to cook, to judge, to learn, to match, to play, to spell, to travel, to watch;* Possible words for participles: *-ed: appeared, approved, climbed, cooked, judged, learned, matched, played, spelled, traveled, watched, worked.*)

Word Tiles *(cont.)*

Procedure *(cont.)*

8. Press the arrow to **advance** to the next page. Tell students that they are going to be shown a sentence that needs one of the three verbals that they have discussed added to the sentence to complete it.

9. **Drag** the pull tab to the left to reveal the sentence to the class. Invite a student to the board and read the sentence to the class.

10. Tell the class that the word in the green box is the verb root of the three verbals listed. One verbal will make the sentence correct. Have students discuss with partners what they think is the correct answer. Invite students to share their answers with the class.

11. Have the student at the board **drag** the correct verbal into the sentence. As a class, read the sentence aloud to check that the correct verbal was chosen (*traveling*).

12. Press the arrow to **advance** to the next page. Continue steps 8–11 for the remaining sentences (*watched, frowning, to laugh*).

13. On their activity sheets, have students choose one of each type of verbal from the first part of the activity and write a sentence using the verbals properly.

Possible Lesson Ideas

The following lesson suggestions can accompany this vocabulary development activity:

- Have students go on a verbal hunt in their reading books. Poll the class to see who could find the most in a given length of time.
- Play Verbal Charades: Verbals are found in many common sayings and phrases (*Seeing is believing!, To be or not to be…, A watched pot never boils*). Create cards with well known verbal sentences or phrases on them. Divide the class into groups and have a representative from each group pick a card. Proceed as you would with any other game of charades.

Interactive Whiteboard File

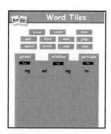  

 # When Is a Verb Not a Verb?

Directions: Complete the map below using the directions from your teacher.

```
                    ┌─────────────────┐
                    │     Verbals     │
                    └─────────────────┘
          ┌──────────────────┼──────────────────┐
  ┌──────────────┐   ┌──────────────┐   ┌──────────────┐
  │    gerund    │   │  infinitive  │   │  participle  │
  └──────────────┘   └──────────────┘   └──────────────┘
```

Used as: _____   _____   _____

Words: _____   _____   _____

       _____   _____   _____

       _____   _____   _____

       _____   _____   _____

       _____   _____   _____

Sentences:

_____

_____

_____

_____

_____

_____

Vocabulary Development Activities

Analyze the Picture

Materials

- Level 6 Interactive Whiteboard File (level6.notebook)
- *Picture Analysis* acivity sheet (p. 52)

Procedure

1. Launch the Level 6 Notebook file by double-clicking on the icon from the Teacher Resource CD. Press the arrow next to Activating Prior Knowledge activities. Begin this activity by pressing on the Analyze the Picture title from the list.

2. Press the arrow to **advance** to the first activity page on the interactive whiteboard. Distribute copies of the *Picture Analysis* activity sheet (p. 52) to students.

3. Tell the class that they are going to observe a picture that relates to something that will be studied in class. Tell the class that the picture is under the four boxes on the screen.

4. Invite a student up to the interactive whiteboard to press the circle that is labeled "1." The box will begin to fade out and a portion of the picture will appear.

5. In the section labeled "1" on their activity sheets, have students list any observations or predictions about the picture.

Interactive Whiteboard Skills

- Advancing pages
- Dragging objects or text

6. **Drag** "Pull Tab 1" out to reveal a question for the class to answer (*What do you observe in the picture?*). Have students share their observations and predictions with the class.

7. Repeat steps 4–6 until the entire picture is revealed and students have responded to each of the questions on the pull tabs.

8. On the lines provided at the bottom of the activity sheet, have students make a prediction about what they think they will be studying next.

9. Once the class has made their predictions and observations, press the arrow to **advance** to the next page.

10. Read the background information to students about the winter at Valley Forge. Have a discussion about the observations that they made about the picture and the information which they just received from the background information.

Analyze the Picture (cont.)

Possible Lesson Ideas

The following lesson suggestions can accompany this activating prior knowledge activity:

- Have students write a descriptive, fictional story regarding what the picture is about.
- Photographs were not available during the Revolutionary War. All of the images that we have are created by artists who made choices about what to include. Have the students think of some recent event that they have witnessed (e.g., a sporting event) and make a written list of the things which they would include if they were artists trying to capture the event for history. How do they decide what to include? How would their own perspective color the way in which they would portray the event?
- Have students each draw the image they planned from the bullet above.

Interactive Whiteboard File

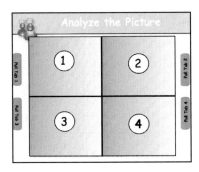

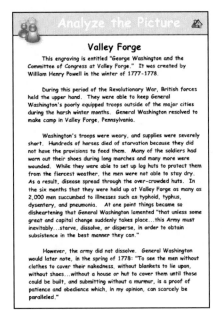

Valley Forge

This engraving is entitled "George Washington and the Committee of Congress at Valley Forge." It was created by William Henry Powell in the winter of 1777-1778.

During this period of the Revolutionary War, British forces held the upper hand. They were able to keep General Washington's poorly equipped troops outside of the major cities during the harsh winter months. General Washington resolved to make camp in Valley Forge, Pennsylvania.

Washington's troops were weary, and supplies were severely short. Hundreds of horses died of starvation because they did not have the provisions to feed them. Many of the soldiers had worn out their shoes during long marches and many more were wounded. While they were able to set up log huts to protect them from the fiercest weather, the men were not able to stay dry. As a result, disease spread through the over-crowded huts. In the six months that they were held up at Valley Forge as many as 2,000 men succumbed to illnesses such as typhoid, typhus, dysentery, and pneumonia. At one point things became so disheartening that General Washington lamented "that unless some great and capital change suddenly takes place...this Army must inevitably...starve, dissolve, or disperse, in order to obtain subsistence in the best manner they can."

However, the army did not dissolve. General Washington would later note, in the spring of 1778: "To see the men without clothes to cover their nakedness, without blankets to lie upon, without shoes...without a house or hut to cover them until those could be built, and submitting without a murmur, is a proof of patience and obedience which, in my opinion, can scarcely be paralleled."

Activating Prior Knowledge Activities

Name: _____

 # Picture Analysis

Directions: Write words or phrases in the boxes below based on what you see in the image displayed on the interactive whiteboard.

1.	**2.**
3.	**4.**

Directions: Make a prediction about what you think you will be studying next.

_____

_____

_____

_____

_____

_____

_____

Anticipation Guide

Materials

- Level 6 Interactive Whiteboard File (level6.notebook)
- *Anticipation Guide* activity sheet (p. 55)
- class set of *Where the Red Fern Grows* by Wilson Rawls (1961)

Interactive Whiteboard Skills

- Advancing pages
- Dragging objects or text
- Using the pen tool

Procedure

1. Launch the Level 6 Notebook file by double-clicking on the icon from the Teacher Resource CD. Press the arrow next to Activating Prior Knowledge activities. Begin this activity by pressing on the Anticipation Guide title from the list.

2. Press the arrow to **advance** to the first activity page on the interactive whiteboard. Distribute copies of the *Anticipation Guide* activity sheet (p. 55) to students.

3. Tell the class that before they read their next story they are going to do some previewing to make predictions about the book, *Where the Red Fern Grows*. Tell students that previewing is a comprehension strategy that helps them set a purpose for reading, and helps them predict what the story may be about.

4. Before showing students the statements that they will be analyzing, have them look at the pictures, title, and other external clues to help gain insight to the story. (***Note:*** Some printings of the book just have cover art and others have more images, so their predictions will depend on which version of the book they have.)

5. After the initial examination, **drag** "Pull Tab 1" out to reveal the first statement. Have students write this statement on their activity sheets.

6. Either as a class, or individually, have students decide if they agree or disagree with that statement based on their current knowledge. Invite a student up to the interactive whiteboard to **drag** either the word *Agree* or *Disagree* from the heading to the appropriate box depending on whether he or she agrees or disagrees with the statement. Discuss the choice as a class.

7. Repeat steps 5 and 6 with the next three pull tabs. Remind students that they must read the book to find out whether they are correct. This gives the students a purpose for reading.

Activating Prior Knowledge Activities

Anticipation Guide (cont.)

Procedure (cont.)

8. After reading the book (this can be done over several days or weeks), discuss the statements on the pull tabs. Either with partners, or as a class, look for the pages in the book that either prove or disprove the four statements. When a useful statement is found, invite a student to the interactive whiteboard to use the **pen tool** and record the page number in the appropriate box.

9. If the class correctly predicted a statement, have a student come up to the interactive whiteboard and **drag** the green check mark to the fourth column box to show that the class's prediction was correct. If the class was incorrect, have the student **drag** the red X to the white square. (**Note:** the check mark and the X are infinitely cloned.)

Possible Lesson Ideas

The following lesson suggestions can accompany this activating prior knowledge activity:

- After writing their next short story in class, have each student prepare an Anticipation Guide for his of her own story. Have students trade stories and complete the guide for their partners' writing.

- Place students in small groups and have them act out their predictions rather than just writing them down. After reading the story, have the groups revise their skits, if needed.

- Have students read a short story individually and create an anticipation guide for another student. Have partners trade anticipation guides and short stories to complete and read independently.

Interactive Whiteboard File

Anticipation Guide

Directions: Write the statements shown on the interactive whiteboard in the appropriate boxes. Write whether you agree or disagree with the statement in the second column of the chart. Finish the chart after reading the book.

Statement	Agree or Disagree	Page Number	Correct (√) or Incorrect (X)

Activating Prior Knowledge Activities

Historical Document

Materials

- Level 6 Interactive Whiteboard File (level6.notebook)
- *Famous Speech* activity sheet (p. 58)

Interactive Whiteboard Skills

- Advancing pages
- Dragging objects or text
- Using the spotlight tool

Procedure

1. Launch the Level 6 Notebook file by double-clicking on the icon from the Teacher Resource CD. Press the arrow next to Activating Prior Knowledge activities. Begin this activity by pressing on the Historical Document title from the list.

2. Press the arrow to **advance** to the first activity page on the interactive whiteboard and distribute copies of the *Famous Speech* activity sheet (p. 58) to students.

3. Tell the class that they are going to review a document from the past and then respond to it in writing. Ask students what they see in the document. Have them record their initial observations on their activity sheets.

4. Invite a student up to the interactive whiteboard to **drag** "Pull Tab 1" from the side of the page. As a class, discuss the question. Look at the physical characteristics of the document.

5. Use the **spotlight tool** to point out specific parts of the document that will help students understand the information in the document more thoroughly. (Possible responses might include: *the preprinted header,*

the date, the fact that it is written on lined paper and in English, the fact that it is hand written with corrections, etc.) Have students record their observations on their activity sheets.

6. Invite another student volunteer to the board to **drag** "Pull Tab 1" back to the side of the page and **drag** "Pull Tab 2" out. Discuss the question and then have students respond to the question on their activity sheets.

7. Have students focus on the specifics of the document's contents. As the document may be difficult for some students to decipher, a transcribed copy of "The Gettysburg Address" is provided on the next page. Press the arrow to **advance** to the next page.

8. Invite student volunteers to read the entire speech and discuss its meaning as a class. Make sure that students are able to understand its archaic sentence structure and references (e.g., *a "score" is a group of 20*). Repeat step 6 until all four questions have been discussed.

Activating Prior Knowledge Activities

Historical Document (cont.)

Procedure

9. After students have finished answering all four questions, assign them to write a positional paragraph describing what they believe to be President Lincoln's main intent in the speech.

Possible Lesson Ideas

The following lesson suggestions can accompany this activating prior knowledge activity:

- Have each student paraphrase the "Gettysburg Address."
- Have students read the "Emancipation Proclamation." Then have students compare and contrast the two documents.
- The "Gettysburg Address" is one of the most famous speeches in history, but it is also among the shortest. Discuss Lincoln's ability to get right to the heart of the matter in a pithy way. As a class, read Lincoln's "Letter to Mrs. Bixby." While it was subsequently discovered that Mrs. Bixby had only lost two of her sons in the war, the letter itself still serves as a monument to brevity. Have the class notice the significance of concise and specific language—short is often best!

Interactive Whiteboard File

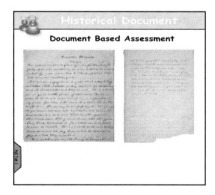

Famous Speech

Directions: Look at the document on the interactive whiteboard and respond to the questions below.

1. Write your initial observations on the lines below.

   _____

   _____

   _____

   _____

2. Pretend you are an anthropologist who is unfamiliar with this document. What can you tell just by looking at it?

   _____

   _____

   _____

3. According to the preprinted header at the top of the paper, when was this document written? Who is the apparent author? How can you tell?

   _____

   _____

4. What point is the author of this speech trying to make? Why?

   _____

   _____

   _____

5. In this short speech, the word *dedicate* (or *dedicated*) is used six times. How is the concept of dedication central to the point?

   _____

   _____

List, Group, Label

Materials

- Level 6 Interactive Whiteboard File (level6.notebook)
- *Vertebrates* activity sheet (p. 61)
- sticky notes

Interactive Whiteboard Skills

- Advancing pages
- Dragging objects or text
- Using the pen tool
- Using the text tool

Procedure

1. Launch the Level 6 Notebook file by double-clicking on the icon from the Teacher Resource CD. Press the arrow next to Activating Prior Knowledge activities. Begin this activity by pressing on the List, Group, Label title from the list.

2. Press the arrow to **advance** to the first activity page on the interactive whiteboard and distribute copies of the *Vertebrates* activity sheet (p. 61) to students.

3. Ask student volunteers to read aloud the terms provided in the box at the top of the screen. Discuss the terms as a class and make sure that students know their meanings.

4. Divide the class into groups of two to four students. Provide each group with sticky notes and have them copy the terms on the sticky notes (one term per sticky note).

5. Allow groups time to organize the terms into different categories. Have students work on desks so they can easily move the sticky notes into the categories chosen. Explain to groups that all of the terms must somehow be included. Students must also record their work on their activity sheets.

6. After the class has placed the sticky notes into categories, select a group to come up to the interactive whiteboard. Then, allow the group to **drag** the terms into the boxes under the labels. The group should be able to justify why it chose to place each term into the various categories. After the group has moved all of the terms, have the class try to guess the names of the categories that the group chose. After several suggestions have been made, have the group use the **pen tool** or the **text tool** to write the category names it chose.

7. Invite a second group to share its ideas using the same procedures as in step 6.

8. Discuss as a class why it is possible to have different categories and still have "correct" answers. Students should begin to see that words could be related differently depending on the categories chosen.

Activating Prior Knowledge Activities

List, Group, Label *(cont.)*

Procedure*(cont.)*

9. Press the arrow to **advance** to the next slide. Explain to students that this represents another way that the terms can be grouped. Discuss how the terms are grouped and make comparisons between this grouping and the others suggested by the students.

Possible Lesson Ideas

The following lesson suggestions can accompany this activating prior knowledge activity:

- Have each student pick a favorite animal, research its full taxonomy, then report back to the class on what each part of the name means.
- Gather up a large group of different kinds of toys. Include games, sports equipment, dolls, video games, etc. Divide students into small groups and challenge them to create a hierarchical categorization process to include each of the objects. Once they are finished, add in some more objects. Do they fit easily into the groups that exist, or do they need to rework their structure?

Interactive Whiteboard File

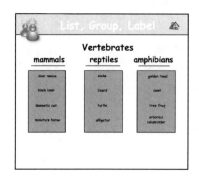

Name:

Vertebrates

Directions: Look at the terms in the box below. Group the terms by how they are related. Then create labels for the categories. Record your ideas in the spaces provided.

Vertebrates		
alligator	domestic cat	newt
arboreal salamander	golden toad	snake
black bear	lizard	tree frog
deer mouse	miniature horse	turtle

Picture Predictions

Materials

- Level 6 Interactive Whiteboard File (level6.notebook)
- *Mathematical Relations* activity sheet (p. 64)

Interactive Whiteboard Skills

- Advancing pages
- Dragging objects or text
- Using the pen tool
- Using the text tool

Procedure

1. Launch the Level 6 Notebook file by double-clicking on the icon from the Teacher Resource CD. Press the arrow next to Activating Prior Knowledge activities. Begin this activity by pressing on the Picture Predictions title from the list.

2. Press the arrow to **advance** to the first activity page on the interactive whiteboard and distribute copies of the *Mathematical Relations* activity sheet (p. 64) to students.

3. Tell the class they are going to observe three pictures. As the pictures are revealed, students will come up with words that can describe all three pictures. In this way, they will decide on the proper mathematical relationship between the objects shown.

4. Have students work with partners or in small groups. Reveal the first picture by pressing on box "1" (*crayon*).

5. Have a student press box "2." Ask students to share how the images relate (e.g., *it is rotated*). Record students' suggestions in the box labeled "Relationship" using the **text tool** or the **pen tool**.

6. Ask a student to **drag** the pull tab under box "3." to reveal a picture. Ask a student to press on the image of the crayon. This will initiate an animation that should give students a final hint as to what the relationship is (*rotation*).

7. Now have the class write a prediction about what all three images have in common. **Drag** the pull tab out to reveal a possible prediction sentence.

8. Press the arrow to **advance** to the next page. Repeat steps 4–7 on this page and see if students can come up with a prediction based on the commonalities of the next three pictures. Students will need a second copy of the *Mathematical Relations* activity sheet (p. 64) in order to complete this part of the activity.

Picture Predictions *(cont.)*

Possible Lesson Ideas

The following lesson suggestions can accompany this activating prior knowledge activity:

- Have students create a piece of art by applying at least three transformations to the letters in their names.
- Transformations are common in the advertisement world. Have students collect ads or other clippings that contain different transformations and create collages using their finds. Optionally, they can group their transformations by type (e.g., dilations, rotations, reflections).

Interactive Whiteboard File

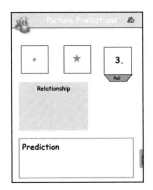

Name:

Mathematical Relations

Directions: Look at the images displayed. Write ways in which the shapes relate to one another. Then, write a prediction about what mathematical relationship describes all three.

Relationship

Relationship

Prediction

Venn Diagram

Materials

- Level 6 Interactive Whiteboard File (level6.notebook)
- *Comparing Societies* activity sheet (p. 67)
- sheet of paper

Interactive Whiteboard Skills

- Advancing pages
- Dragging objects or text
- Using the pen tool
- Using the text tool

Procedure

1. Launch the Level 6 Notebook file by double-clicking on the icon from the Teacher Resource CD. Press the arrow next to Graphic Organizer activities. Begin this activity by pressing on the Venn Diagram title from the list.

2. Press the arrow to **advance** to the first activity page on the interactive whiteboard and distribute copies of the *Comparing Societies* activity sheet (p. 67) to students.

3. Tell the class that they are going to write essays comparing Hunter-Gatherer and Agrarian societies. They are going to find common traits between societies and traits that are specific to each society.

4. Tell students that before they start writing, they must first organize their thoughts and ideas onto a graphic organizer (Venn diagram). This step of the writing process is known as the prewrite.

5. Select a student to come up to the interactive whiteboard and use the **pen tool** or the **text tool** to write the words *Hunter-Gatherer* at the top of the circle on the left and the word

Agrarian at the top of the circle on the right. Have the rest of the class fill out their own Venn diagrams.

6. As a class, discuss the sections of the Venn diagram and ask students what type of information belongs in each section. Make sure students clearly understand that the common traits of Hunter-Gatherer and Agrarian societies will go in the middle section.

7. As a class, read the words and phrases found below the Venn diagram. Make sure students understand what each word/phrase means.

8. Allow students time to discuss which words or phrases belong in the middle of the diagram. Then invite a student to the interactive whiteboard and have him or her **drag** the appropriate traits into the middle section. Discuss with the class why these traits belong in the middle section (*engaged in trade, used tools, buried their dead, domesticated animals, wove cloth*). Have students record these traits on their activity sheets.

Venn Diagram *(cont.)*

Procedure *(cont.)*

9. Repeat step 8 for the traits that only pertain to Hunter-Gatherer societies (*moved with the seasons, camped close to their food, lived in small bands, nomadic*).

10. Repeat step 8 for the traits that only pertain to Agrarian societies (*built permanent homes, domesticated animals, formed large communities, settled in one place, vulnerable to raiders*).

11. Once the Venn diagrams are completed, have students begin to write their essays on separate sheets of paper.

12. As students write, remind them to refer back to their Venn diagrams in order to keep themselves organized and to remember all of the traits.

Possible Lesson Ideas

The following lesson suggestions can accompany this graphic organizer activity:

• Once students' essays are complete, have them switch with partners and work at editing/revising their work.

• Continue to use the Venn diagram technique to compare and contrast societies throughout other social studies units (e.g., Greek versus Roman, Ancient Egyptian versus Ancient Chinese).

Interactive Whiteboard File

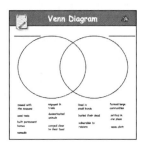

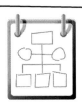

Comparing Societies

Directions: Write words to compare two topics as instructed by your teacher.

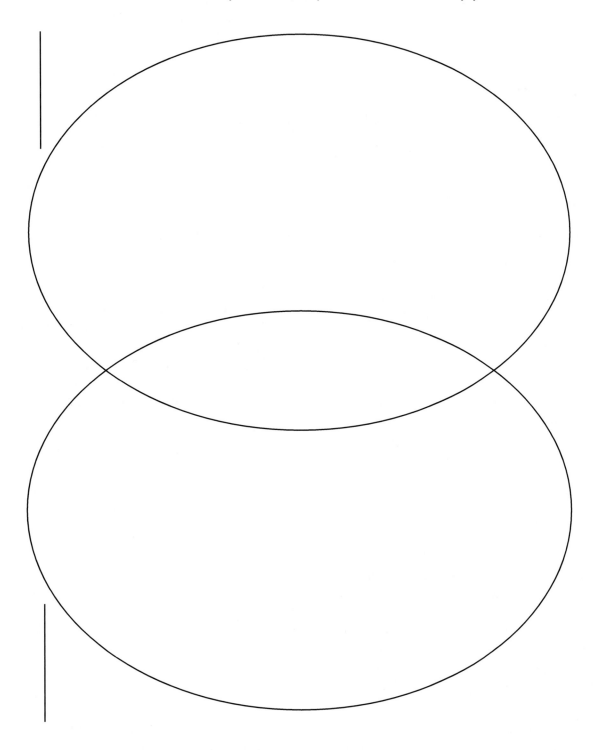

Graphic Organizer Activities

Flow Chart

Materials

- Level 6 Interactive Whiteboard File (level6.notebook)
- *Order of Operations* activity sheet (p. 70)

Procedure

1. Launch the Level 6 Notebook file by double-clicking on the icon from the Teacher Resource CD. Press the arrow next to Graphic Organizer activities. Begin this activity by pressing on the Flow Chart title from the list.

2. Press the arrow to **advance** to the first activity page on the interactive whiteboard and distribute copies of the *Order of Operations* activity sheet (p. 70) to students.

3. Tell students that today they are going to create a set of written instructions in sequential order. Tell them that they are going to list the steps involved in solving an arithmetic problem using Order of Operations.

4. Explain that a flow chart is a step-by-step illustration of a specific event.

5. Invite a student up to the interactive whiteboard to **drag** the red star to the left to see one of the steps. Discuss with the class where the step might go in the flow chart. Tell the class that they can move the step later if they think it needs to be adjusted as they see more of the process.

Interactive Whiteboard Skills

- Advancing pages
- Dragging objects or text
- Using the pen tool
- Using the text tool

6. Once the class has decided where the first step should go, have the student **drag** it to the appropriate box.

7. Repeat steps 5 and 6 until all of the steps are placed on the flow chart.

8. Have students tell partners the correct sequential steps in the Order of Operations. Make sure that students understand that multiplication and division are in the same step and should be worked left to right. The same is true for addition and subtraction. They should NOT prioritize multiplication over division or addition over subtraction.

9. Tell the class that now that they have the general rules in order, they are going to place a specific problem in order on the flow chart. Press the arrow to **advance** to the next page.

Flow Chart *(cont.)*

Procedure *(cont.)*

10. Invite a student up to the interactive whiteboard to **drag** the red star to the left to see the first mathematical sentence or expression. As a class, discuss and decide where this sentence should go on the flow chart.

11. Once the class has decided where the first mathematical or expression sentence should go, have the student **drag** it to the appropriate box.

12. Repeat steps 10 and 11 until all of the sentences and expressions are placed on the flow chart.

13. Once they all are placed, have students record the sentences and expressions on their activity sheets.

Possible Lesson Ideas

The following lesson suggestions can accompany this graphic organizer activity:

- Have students create their own mnemonic for Order of Operations. A popular mnemonic is, "*Pandas Eat Mustard on Dumplings and Apples with Spice.*" This helps remind students that the multiplication and division steps are grouped, as are addition and subtraction.

- Have students create their own Order of Operations problems and trade with partners. Allow them to use their flow charts to aid in solving the problems.

- Have students create their own flow charts for a different mathematical procedure in which they feel they need help remembering the steps.

Interactive Whiteboard File

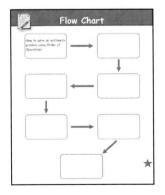 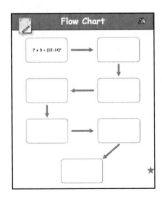

Name:

Order of Operations

Directions: Complete the flow chart according to your teacher's directions.

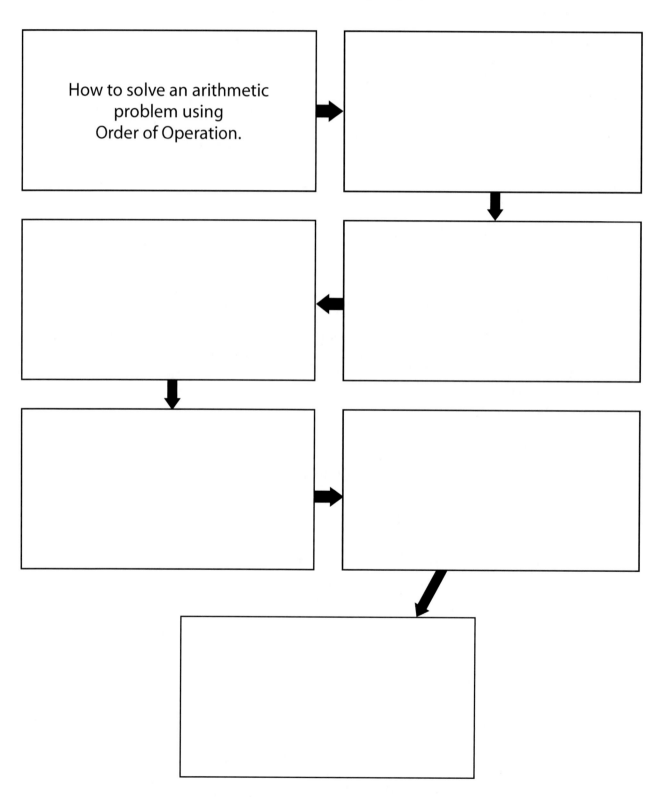

How to solve an arithmetic
problem using
Order of Operation.

KWL Chart

Materials

- Level 6 Interactive Whiteboard File (level6.notebook)
- *My KWL* activity sheet (p. 73)
- sheet of paper

Procedure

1. Launch the Level 6 Notebook file by double-clicking on the icon from the Teacher Resource CD. Press the arrow next to Graphic Organizer activities. Begin this activity by pressing on the KWL Chart title from the list.

2. Press the arrow to **advance** to the first activity page on the interactive whiteboard and distribute copies of the *My KWL* activity sheet (p. 73) to students. Tell students that KWL charts can be used to help organize the information which you know about a topic for research and brainstorm things you want to know and plan to learn more about. Tell students that you are going to do a sample as a class before allowing them to create their own KWL charts on a research topic of their choice. Slide the **screen shade** down to show the KWL title and the topic, "Life in Ancient Greece."

3. Tell the class that they are going to plan how to research ancient Greece using a KWL chart. Review each initial with the class explaining that the "K" stands for what we *k*now about ancient Greece. The "W" stands for what we *w*ant to learn or research and the "L" stands for what we *l*earned from the research.

Interactive Whiteboard Skills

- Advancing pages
- Using the pen tool
- Using the screen shade
- Using the text tool

4. Slide the **screen shade** down until the first box ("What do I *Know*") is revealed. Ask the class to brainstorm about ancient Greece. Use the **pen tool** or the **text tool** to record the students' suggestions about what they know about ancient Greece in the first box. Do not be concerned if the statement is true or not.
Tip: To control the management of all students wanting to share, use a soft ball or stuffed animal. Only the student who has possession of the object can share.

5. Slide the **screen shade** down until the middle box ("What do I *Want* to know") is revealed. Record questions students have about what life was like in ancient Greece. To give ownership to the questions being recorded, write students' initials next to their questions.

6. Ask the class what resources could be used to help find out the answers to the questions on the chart. Have students record the resources suggested on a separate sheet of paper. Some examples might be a book, the Internet, videos, or a magazine.

KWL Chart *(cont.)*

Procedure *(cont.)*

7. Using one or more of the resources listed, try to answer some of the questions students have posed for the class. Once an answer has been found, slide the **screen shade** all the way down to reveal the last box ("What have I *Learned*?") for the class. Tell students that the last box is for the answers they have found to the questions. Record this information in the last box.

8. Discuss how this information could be used to help students plan to write a research paper. Then allow students to begin recording information on their own activity sheets to plan their research on whatever topic has been assigned to them or that they have chosen.

Possible Lesson Ideas

The following lesson suggestions can accompany this graphic organizer activity:

- Have students complete their own research based on the topics which they began thinking about. Allow students to research their questions and create a report on their topic.

- Have students complete their own research based on the topics which they began thinking about. Allow students to research their questions and show what they have learned in a creative writing assignment of their choice (e.g., poem, short story, graphic novel).

Interactive Whiteboard File

Name: _____

My KWL

Directions: Record the information for your research on the KWL chart below.

Life in Ancient Greece

What do I *Know*?

What do I *Want* to know?

What have I *Learned*?

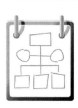

T-Chart

Graphic Organizer Activities

Materials

- Level 6 Interactive Whiteboard File (level6.notebook)
- *Verb Agreement* activity sheet (p. 76)

Procedure

1. Launch the Level 6 Notebook file by double-clicking on the icon from the Teacher Resource CD. Press the arrow next to Graphic Organizer activities. Begin this activity by pressing on the T-Chart title from the list.

2. Press the arrow to **advance** to the first activity page on the interactive whiteboard and distribute copies of *Verb Agreement* activity sheet (p. 76) to students.

3. Tell the class that today they are going to use what they know about verb agreement to make a subject and verb agree. As a class, discuss the information provided on the T-chart.

4. Tell the class that the T-chart will help keep the information organized.

Interactive Whiteboard Skills

- Advancing pages
- Dragging objects or text
- Using the pen tool

5. Select a student to come up to the interactive whiteboard and **drag** the red star into the "Subject" column (*Stephanie and Martha*) to align with the first verb (*to run*). Then have the student use the **pen tool** to write a form of the verb that will agree with the subject. (*Stephanie and Martha run.*)

6. As a class, check the volunteer's work and then have students write the corresponding information on their activity sheets.

7. Repeat steps 4–6 for the remaining verbs on the chart. (*Jason grows; the turtles are; several summers begin; five of my favorite people have; Yosemite survives; a student learns*).

8. At the bottoms of their pages, have students each write a sentence for each of the verb-subject combinations on the chart.

T-Chart *(cont.)*

Possible Lesson Ideas

The following lesson suggestions can accompany this graphic organizer activity:

- Have students add a helping verb to each subject-verb combination when they write their sentences.
- Divide the class into two groups. Have one group create cards with verbs on them, and the other group create cards with subjects. Shuffle the cards and deal out five of each card to each student. Have students create sentences with their cards.

Interactive Whiteboard File

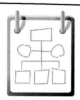

Verb Agreement

Directions: Use the T-chart below to record the verb, the subject, and the form of the verb that agrees with the subject. Then use each subject and verb in a sentence.

Verb	Subject	Verb Form that Agrees with the Subject

1. _____

2. _____

3. _____

4. _____

5. _____

6. _____

7. _____

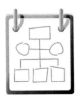

Web Map

Materials

- Level 6 Interactive Whiteboard File (level6.notebook)
- *Eukaryote Web* activity sheet (p. 79)

Interactive Whiteboard Skills

- Advancing pages
- Pinning pages (*optional*)
- Using dual page display (*optional*)
- Using the pen tool
- Using the text tool

Procedure

1. Launch the Level 6 Notebook file by double-clicking on the icon from the Teacher Resource CD. Press the arrow next to Graphic Organizer activities. Begin this activity by pressing on the Web Map title from the list.

2. Press the arrow to **advance** to the first activity page on the interactive whiteboard and distribute several copies of the *Eukaryote Web* activity sheet (p. 79) to students.

3. Tell the class that they are going to learn about different types of eukaryotes and use a technique called brainstorming to see what we already know about eukaryotes and then make connections between our ideas. Make sure that everyone knows that eukaryotes are the domain of life forms with cells that include a membrane, a nucleus, and several organelles.

4. Have students write the word *eukaryote* in the bubble on their activity sheets. Brainstorm different qualities of eukaryotes and use the **pen tool** or the **text tool** to write these ideas in the web. Press the arrow to **advance** to the next page.

5. Ask the class if anyone can identify the type of eukaryote shown. Invite a student to the interactive whiteboard to use the **pen tool** or **text tool** to write the name (*protist)* in the center oval. Have students also add this to one of their activity sheets. Ask the class to brainstorm about *protists*. The students may describe the characteristics, give specific examples, compare it to something else, or share anything else they might know about *protists*. Use the **pen tool** or the **text tool** to record students' ideas. Also have students add these ideas to their activity sheets stemming from the bubble in which they wrote the word *protist*.

Web Map *(cont.)*

Procedure *(cont.)*

6. Press the arrow to **advance** to the next page. Repeat step 5 until students have brainstormed about each type of eukaryote (*fungi, plants, animals*).

7. Have students share the connections they made between the eukaryotes. Encourage them to observe similarities or differences between them. Use the **dual page display** and **pin page** functions to compare two eukaryote webs together on the interactive whiteboard. (**Pin page** is listed under "View" in the "Zoom" submenu.) Add more bubbles, if necessary, to fill in more information about each kingdom.

Possible Lesson Ideas

The following lesson suggestions can accompany this graphic organizer activity:

- Have students create a matching game by drawing the different eukaryotes on index cards. On another set of index cards, have them write the names and characteristics of the eukaryotes and play against a partner.

- Read different "clues" about a particular eukaryote and see if students can infer which type you are describing. Start with general clues and gradually have them get more specific.

Interactive Whiteboard File

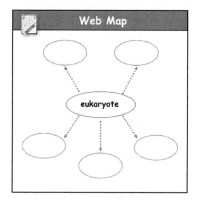
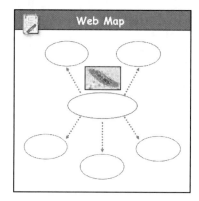
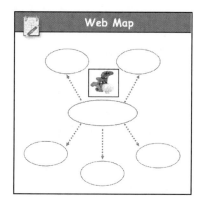

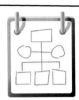

Eukaryote Web

Directions: Use the information your classmates share to create web maps about eukaryotes.

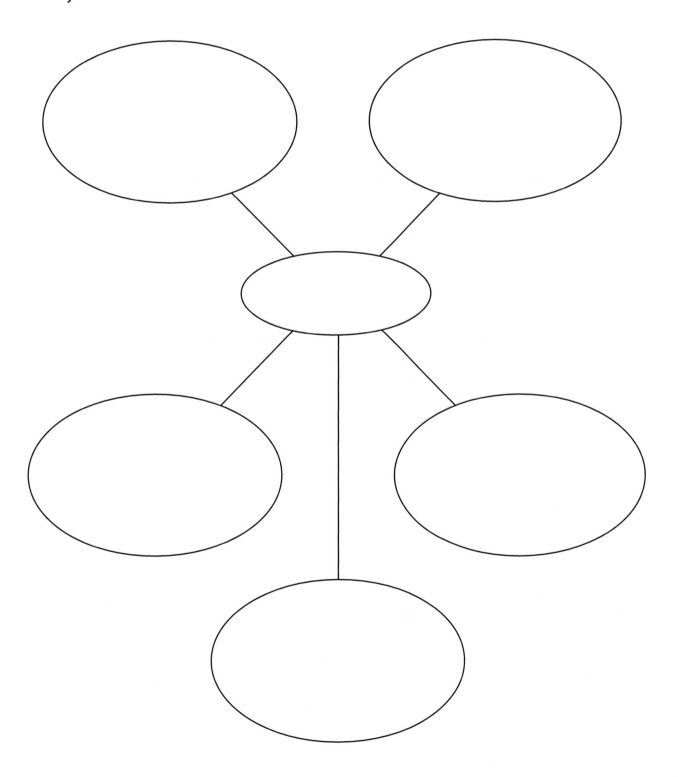

Cause and Effect

Materials

- Level 6 Interactive Whiteboard File (level6.notebook)
- *Causes and Effects* activity sheet (p. 82)

Interactive Whiteboard Skills

- Advancing pages
- Dragging objects or text

Procedure

1. Launch the Level 6 Notebook file by double-clicking on the icon from the Teacher Resource CD. Press the arrow next to Comprehension activities. Begin this activity by pressing on the *Cause and Effect* title from the list.

2. Before the lesson starts, prop a book up with something unsteady. Press the arrow to **advance** to the first activity page on the interactive whiteboard and distribute copies of the *Causes and Effects* activity sheet (p. 82) to students. As you distribute the activity sheets, intentionally bump into the book so that it falls over. This will get the students' attention. Discuss with the class what happened and why it happened.

3. Remind the class that when something happens, there is always a cause and effect. A cause is what makes something happen. To find the cause, you need to ask yourself, "What happened first?" (*The book was unsteady, or bumping into the book is the cause.*)

4. Now ask the class what happened as the result (*the book fell over*). Explain that an effect is what happens because of something else (the cause). To find the effect, you need to ask yourself, "What happened second?" and "Would it have happened if the first thing had not ocurred?"

5. Direct students' attention to the interactive whiteboard and read the first cause to the class. (*Drop a cup on the ground.*) Have the class predict what might be the effect. After discussing some possible effects, invite a student up to the interactive whiteboard and have the student **drag** the cause through the "Magic Tunnel" to reveal a possible effect (*the cup breaks*). The image on the left side of the page can help give a visual of cause and effect.

6. Repeat step 5 with the remaining sentences and images on the page. Discuss the relationship between the causes and effects.

7. Press the arrow to **advance** to the next page. Remind the class that they have been studying the Rock Cycle.

Cause and Effect *(cont.)*

Procedure *(cont.)*

8. Read the first cause to the class and have them record it on their activity sheets (*Layers of sediment build up over millions of years*). Discuss some possible effects that could have taken place. There can be many correct answers as long as the student can justify it.

9. Invite a student up to the interactive whiteboard to **drag** the effect through the "Magic Tunnel" to reveal a possible effect. Have students record this on their activity sheets.

10. Repeat steps 8 and 9 until all of the effects have been revealed.

Possible Lesson Ideas

The following lesson suggestions can accompany this comprehension activity:

- Take samples of several types of rock. Allow students to examine them and then make predictions about which rocks will change the most when exposed to freezing. Put each rock in a plastic bag or other freezer-safe container. Cover each in water and then freeze. Allow them to thaw. Repeat this process 5–10 times, then re-examine the rocks. Which ones have changed the most? Can you observe little pieces of rock that have broken off? Were students' predictions correct?

- Have students make a dioramic model of the rock cycle.

- Take a field trip to a rock quarry or local rock formations.

Interactive Whiteboard File

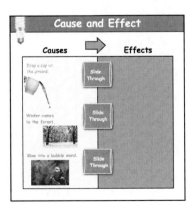

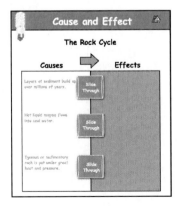

Name: _____

Causes and Effects

Directions: Record the causes and effects on the chart below according to the directions from your teacher.

Cause	Effect

Classify and Categorize

Materials

- Level 6 Interactive Whiteboard File (level6.notebook)
- *What To Do with Shapes* activity sheet (p. 85)
- construction paper
- scissors
- glue sticks

Interactive Whiteboard Skills

- Advancing pages
- Dragging objects or text
- Using the eraser
- Using the pen tool

Procedure

1. Launch the Level 6 Notebook file by double-clicking on the icon from the Teacher Resource CD. Press the arrow next to Comprehension activities. Begin this activity by pressing on the Classify and Categorize title from the list.

2. Press the arrow to **advance** to the first activity page on the interactive whiteboard and distribute copies of the *What To Do with Shapes* activity sheet (p. 85) to students. Allow students time to cut out the shapes on the page.

3. Tell the class that they are going to classify geometric shapes into three categories. Tell them that they are going to look at each shape and see if there are any with shared characteristics.

4. Have students work with partners to classify the shapes. Try not to give too much help or suggest classifications to your students. Let them discover these on their own. Have students move their shapes on their desks into three categories.

5. Invite a pair of students up to the interactive whiteboard to **drag** the shapes on the board according to how they sorted them on their desks and use the **pen tool** to write the categories at the top of the chart. As a class, discuss how the shapes were sorted and have pairs raise their hands if they sorted the same way.

6. **Drag** the shapes out of the chart and use the **eraser** to **erase** the text within the chart. Invite one or two other pairs to repeat steps 5 and 6.

7. Press the arrow to **advance** to the next page. Distribute a sheet of construction paper to each student and have students fold the paper into thirds.

8. Read the categories at the top of the chart and have students label their papers the same way. Then allow students time to look at the relationships between the shapes.

Comprehension Activities

Classify and Categorize (cont.)

Procedure (cont.)

9. Invite a student up to the interactive whiteboard to **drag** the shapes with equal sides into the correct section. Have students do the same with the shapes at their desks and glue them to the construction paper. Repeat this procedure for the remaining two sections.

Possible Lesson Ideas

The following lesson suggestions can accompany this comprehension activity:

- Have each student pick a shape and then find and record as many real-world occurrences of that shape as they can in 24 hours. Some shapes are easier to find than others, so put an upper limit of 30–50 depending on your class. Compare lists the next day.
- Provide students with a variety of geometric shapes of various colors and have students assemble them into mosaic images.
- Assemble other objects that can be sorted in a variety of ways (blocks, noodles, art supplies, seashells, etc.) and challenge students to sort the objects into categories.

Interactive Whiteboard File

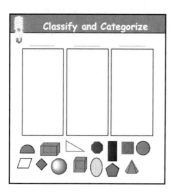
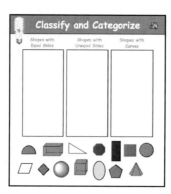

Name:

What To Do with Shapes

Directions: Cut out the shapes below. Sort them according to the directions from your teacher.

Shapes with Equal Sides	Shapes with Unequal Sides	Shapes with Curves

Comprehension Activities

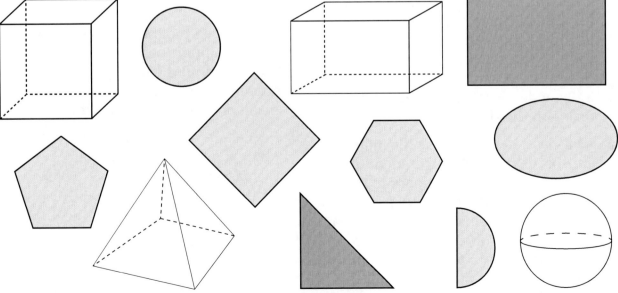

Main Idea and Details

Materials

- Level 6 Interactive Whiteboard File (level6.notebook)
- *Monochromatic Ink Brush Painting* activity sheet (p. 88)
- sheet of paper

Interactive Whiteboard Skills

- Advancing pages
- Using dual page display
- Using the highlighting tool
- Using the pen tool
- Using the text tool

Procedure

1. Launch the Level 6 Notebook file by double-clicking on the icon from the Teacher Resource CD. Press the arrow next to Comprehension activities. Begin this activity by pressing on the Main Idea and Details title from the list.

2. Press the arrow to **advance** to the first activity page on the interactive whiteboard and distribute copies of the *Monochromatic Ink Brush Painting* activity sheet (p. 88) to students.

3. Have a student read the title of the passage to the class.

4. Depending on the level of your students, choose how to best read the text aloud. Some possible choices include: echo read, choral read, teacher reads aloud independently, or student volunteers read aloud independently. Read the complete text with the students.

5. As a class, decide what is the main idea of the text. Invite a student up to the interactive whiteboard to use the **highlighting tool** to **highlight** the sentence that helps tell the main idea of the passage: *Monochromatic ink brush painting is a traditional Asian art form.*

6. Press the arrow to **advance** to the next page. Use the **pen tool** or the **text tool** to write the main idea in the center of the organizer. Have students also record the main idea on their activity sheets.

7. Use **dual page display** to show the passage and the graphic organizer together. Read the second paragraph aloud to the class. Discuss the paragraph, as a class, and see if there are any details that support the main idea. Invite a student up to the interactive whiteboard to use the **pen tool** or the **highlighting tool** to underline or highlight the supporting details.

8. Use the **pen tool** or the **text tool** to write a supporting detail in one of the four boxes on the organizer. Have students also record the supporting detail on their activity sheets.

9. Repeat steps 6–8 to choose three other supporting details from the passage.

Comprehension Activities

Main Idea and Details *(cont.)*

Procedure *(cont.)*

10. Have students summarize the passage on a new sheet of paper using the main ideas and supporting details they recorded on their activity sheets.

Possible Lesson Ideas

The following lesson suggestions can accompany this comprehension activity:

- Show students examples of Japanese and Chinese ink brush art. Using black watercolors and brushes, have students create their own monochromatic brush art.

- Ink brush art is sometimes called a "Haiku in visual form." Study Japanese Haiku and have students create their own poems.

- Common symbols in sumi-e include plum trees, orchids, bamboo, chrysanthemum, and pine trees. These are plants that are common to the region and hold cultural significance. As a class, brainstorm wildlife or items that are common in your area and might have cultural significance. Have students use these symbols in their art and poetry.

Interactive Whiteboard File

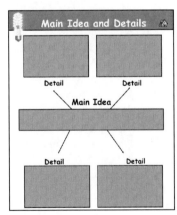

Comprehension Activities

Monochromatic Ink Brush Painting

Directions: Add the main idea and supporting details from the passage read aloud in class.

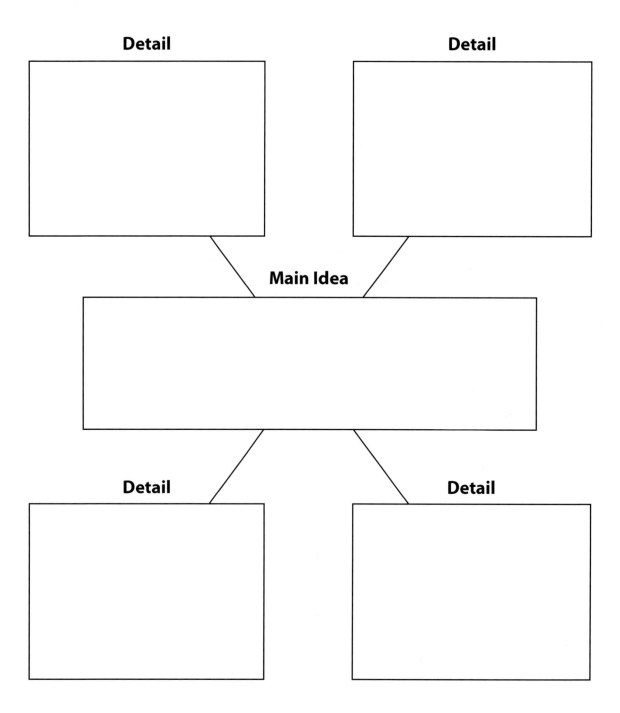

Detail

Detail

Main Idea

Detail

Detail

Sequencing

Materials

- Level 6 Interactive Whiteboard File (level6.notebook)
- *Flashing Back into Sequence* activity sheet (p. 91)

Interactive Whiteboard Skills

- Advancing pages
- Dragging objects or text
- Using dual page display
- Using the highlighting tool
- Using the pen tool
- Using the text tool

Procedure

1. Launch the Level 6 Notebook file by double-clicking on the icon from the Teacher Resource CD. Press the arrow next to Comprehension activities. Begin this activity by pressing on the Sequencing title from the list.

2. Press the arrow to **advance** to the first activity page on the interactive whiteboard and distribute copies of the *Flashing Back into Sequence* activity sheet (p. 91) to students.

3. Ask students to list what they know about *flashbacks*. Use the **pen tool** or the **text tool** to brainstorm ideas about flashbacks in the blue box on the interactive whiteboard. (*Students should focus on the idea that flashbacks are a literary technique used to show something that happened before the current events.*)

4. Press the arrow to **advance** to the next page. Read the passage aloud to students. Have them listen for the flashback section as you read.

5. Invite student volunteers up to the interactive whiteboard to use the **pen tool** to circle the flashback section. Have another student **highlight** the sentences that indicate that the text is moving into and out of the flashback section (*"He remembered one summer day in particular"* and *"Gerald was roused from his memory by a yawn from his wife"*).

6. Press the arrow to **advance** to the next page. Tell the class that they are going to use this sequence chart to help put the events of the passage in the correct order. Remind students that the events in the flashback actually happened *before* the events in the main part of the passage.

Comprehension Activities

Sequencing (cont.)

Procedure (cont.)

7. Invite a student up to the interactive whiteboard and have him or her **drag** the blue star to the right to reveal an event from the story. Discuss as a class where the event should be placed on the sequencing chart. Remind the students that they may decide to move the event later.

8. Repeat step 7 until all of the events have been placed on the sequencing chart. If students are struggling, press the **dual page display** so you can see the story alongside the sequencing chart. Once the chart is complete, have students complete their activity sheets.

Possible Lesson Ideas

The following lesson suggestions can accompany this comprehension activity:

- Have each student find three examples of flashbacks in stories that they have read. Let them pick their favorite to share with the class.
- Have students write their own stories using flashbacks.
- Divide the class into groups. After reading a story to the class, place the events of the story on different pieces of paper, one event per sheet. Give one event to each student in the group. Have the group work together to stand in the correct sequence.

Interactive Whiteboard File

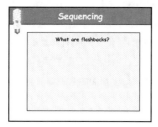

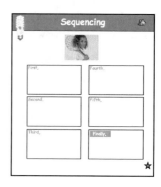

Flashing Back into Sequence

Directions: Write the events in order according to the story read aloud to the class.

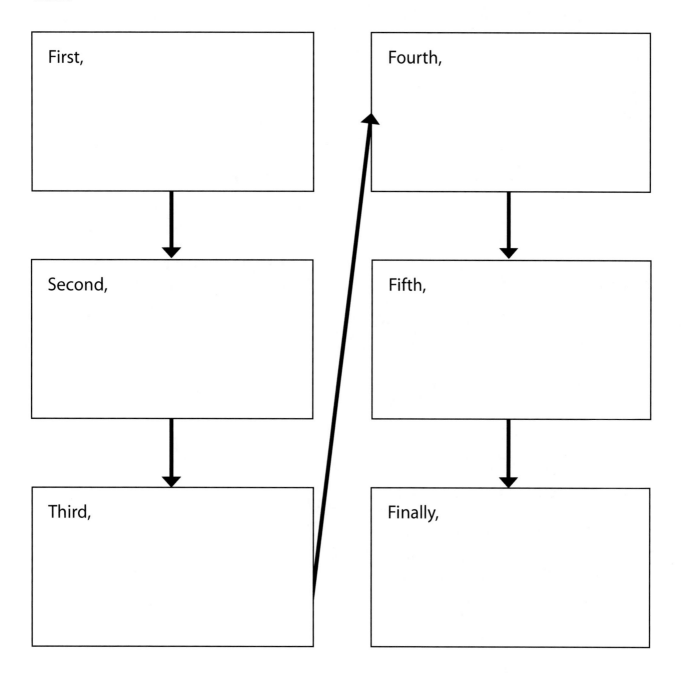

First,

Second,

Third,

Fourth,

Fifth,

Finally,

Summarizing

Comprehension Activities

Materials

- Level 6 Interactive Whiteboard File (level6.notebook)
- *Story Summary* activity sheet (p. 94)
- short, familiar piece of children's literature
- sheet of paper

Interactive Whiteboard Skills

- Advancing pages
- Using the pen tool
- Using the spotlight tool
- Using the text tool

Procedure

1. Launch the Level 6 Notebook file by double-clicking on the icon from the Teacher Resource CD. Press the arrow next to Comprehension activities. Begin this activity by pressing on the Summarizing title from the list.

2. Press the arrow to **advance** to the first activity page on the interactive whiteboard and distribute copies of the *Story Summary* activity sheet (p. 94) to students.

3. Introduce the selected piece of children's literature and then read it aloud to students.

4. Review the different parts of the summary chart with students. Reread the story and have students fill in parts of their activity sheets as they hear them discussed in the story.

5. As a class, discuss each section of the chart. Use the **pen tool** or the **text tool** to record students' ideas. Allow students to edit their charts throughout the class discussion.

6. Review the completed chart using the **spotlight tool** to point out each section of the chart.

7. Have students use the summary chart to write a one-paragraph summary of the story on their own papers. Invite students to share their completed summaries orally with the class.

Summarizing *(cont.)*

Possible Lesson Ideas

The following lesson suggestions can accompany this comprehension activity:

- Have students create three sets of cards with generic characters (e.g., *a dog, a police officer, a dandelion salesman*), settings (e.g., *a farm, the space station, Far Far Away*), and problems (e.g., *someone has lost their mittens, a dragon is coming, the birthday cake was dropped*) written on them. Have the students each pick two or three characters, a setting, and a problem, then fill in the summary charts with the story starters they have selected. Next, have them plan the rest of their stories by filling in the chart with four events and a solution. Finally, have them write the stories they created.

- Read a chapter book to the class and assign each chapter to a student. Have each student draw a picture of the most important event in his or her chapter and write a summary for that chapter. Once everyone is finished with his or her summary, create a class book.

Interactive Whiteboard File

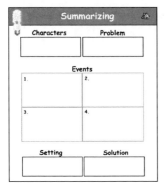

Story Summary

Directions: Complete the chart below to summarize the story read aloud to the class.

Characters	Problem

Events

Setting	Solution

Content Links

Materials

- Level 6 Interactive Whiteboard File (level6.notebook)
- index cards
- markers
- *Linking Matter* activity sheet (p. 97)

Procedure

1. Launch the Level 6 Notebook file by double-clicking on the icon from the Teacher Resource CD. Press the arrow next to Review activities. Begin this activity by pressing on the Content Links title from the list.

2. Write the terms from the first activity page on the index cards, one term per card. There should be one term for each student in the class. This activity may also be done with partners if there are not enough terms available.

3. Press the arrow to **advance** to the first activity page on the interactive whiteboard and tell the class that they are going to do a review activity on the nature of matter. Students should be familiar with these terms before starting this review activity. For struggling students and/or English language learners, you may review the terms with drawings or gestures.

4. Distribute one index card to each student (or pair). Have each student read his or her term out loud to the class. Discuss the term as a class and review its meaning.

Interactive Whiteboard Skills

- Advancing pages
- Dragging objects or text
- Using the pen tool

5. Tell the class that they will each circulate around the room with their terms, looking for a student who has another term that has a connection or a link with theirs. Remind the class that there is more than one correct answer. Have students discuss how and why their terms are linked together.

6. Have students come up to the interactive whiteboard and **drag** their terms together so that they are now linked on the board. Have students select the **pen tool** and write their initials next to their linked terms. After they have linked their terms together, have them sit or stand together until the rest of the class have finished linking their terms.

7. Ask each pair to explain why they chose to link their two terms together. If students could not find a person with whom to link, they may stand by themselves and then tell the class why their term could not be linked. Ask the class how to link the terms to make groups of three terms. Mirror those choices on the interactive whiteboard by **dragging** the appropriate terms together.

Review Activities

Content Links *(cont.)*

Procedure *(cont.)*

8. Once all the groups have had a chance to share, collect the index cards and have students return to their desks. Distribute copies of the *Linking Matter* activity sheet (p. 97) to students. Have students choose four linked pairs from the interactive whiteboard and write the terms in the boxes at the top of their activity sheets. Allow them time to write at least two sentences about the relationship between each pair of terms.

9. If you would like to have students play again, **drag** the terms apart on the interactive whiteboard and distribute the index cards again. Tell the class that they are going to do the same activity but with different terms. Remind them that they may not link with the same term from the previous round. Repeat steps 5–7 with the class. As a group, discuss why the same terms can be linked in different ways.

Possible Lesson Ideas

The following lesson suggestions can accompany this review activity:

- Matter is mostly made of space. Have students conduct a demonstration of this. Fill a plastic cup to the rim with hot water. Fill it so that the water is domed—almost overflowing. Now measure a teaspoon full of powdered sugar. Ask students to predict how many teaspoons of sugar can be added before the water overflows. Add the sugar to the water. Do not touch the spoon to the water or stir. The water will not overflow because the sugar is dissolving and filling in the spaces in the water. Add more teaspoons full of sugar until the space is so saturated that the water does eventually overflow.

- Have students build models of atoms out of recycled objects found around the house.

Interactive Whiteboard File

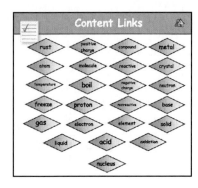

Linking Matter

Directions: Choose four sets of linked terms from the interactive whiteboard and write them in the boxes below. Write a sentence or two about how the terms are related.

Terms:	**Terms:**

Terms:	**Terms:**

_____

_____

_____

_____

_____

_____

_____

_____

_____

Review Activities

Game Board

Materials

- Level 6 Interactive Whiteboard File (level6.notebook)
- *Review Game* activity sheet (p. 100)

Procedure

1. Launch the Level 6 Notebook file by double-clicking on the icon from the Teacher Resource CD. Press the arrow next to Review activities. Begin this activity by pressing on the Game Board title from the list.

2. Tell the class that they are going to do an activity to help them review *simile, metaphor, hyperbole,* and *alliteration.* Students should already have an understanding of these types of figurative language and have had some practice in identifying them and applying them in sentences.

3. Press the arrow to **advance** to the first activity page on the interactive whiteboard and divide the class into five groups. Distribute copies of the *Review Game* activity sheet (p. 100) to each student.

4. Have students look at the spinner in the upper right hand corner of the page. Demonstrate to the class how to press the middle of the spinner to make it spin. Spin the spinner and review the types of figurative language as the spinner lands on each of them. Ask for some examples and use them in sentences. Do this for all four types of figurative language.

Interactive Whiteboard Skills

- Advancing pages
- Dragging objects or text

5. Tell students that they will be working together as teams. Their goal is to move their game pieces (ship, plane, scooter, balloon, helicopter, or car) from the start area to the "Finish" flags. They must also use their charts to record the types of figurative language that are landed on throughout the game.

6. To start the game, assign each group a game piece that is on the interactive whiteboard. That game piece will represent its table or group. Select a student from the group who will go up first to the interactive whiteboard.

7. Have the student press the spinner. Once the spinner stops, have the student confer with his or her group to find the first example on the game board of that type of figurative language. (***Note:*** Some answers are examples of more than one type. For example, "the pill was as large as a grapefruit" is both a *hyperbole* and a *simile.*) Allow about 20 seconds for the group to come to consensus. Then have the student **drag** the group's assigned game piece to the first example on the path (e.g., if the spinner lands on "Alliteration," the student will **drag** the game piece to the phrase, "Peter Piper picked a peck of pickled peppers").

Review Activities

Game Board *(cont.)*

Procedure *(cont.)*

8. Have the class decide whether the group moved to the correct space. Then have the class record the chosen word on their activity sheets in the appropriate column. For example, students would record the phrase *Peter Piper picked a peck of pickled peppers* in the "Alliteration" column.

9. Select a student from the second group to come up to the interactive whiteboard and press the spinner. Have this group follow the same procedures as the first group to determine where it should move its game piece. Continue with the rest of the groups, going in the same order.

10. To win the game, the group must reach the "Finish" flag. If the group spins the spinner and there are no more parts of speech in front of it, it will cross the "Finish" and win the game. Another way to play is for the groups to go to the "Finish" and then back to the "Start" on the game board to win the game.

Possible Lesson Ideas

The following lesson suggestions can accompany this review activity:

- Distribute blank game boards and have students create their own games by adding their own examples of the different types of figurative language. Have students play each other's games as a center or workstation activity.
- Have students collect examples of figurative language from their reading over the course of two weeks. Share the examples and display them in the room.

Interactive Whiteboard File

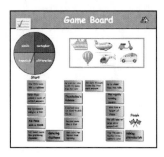

Review Game

Directions: Once a team lands on a phrase, record it in the correct category in the chart below.

Simile	Metaphor	Hyperbole	Alliteration

Review Activities

Guess It!

Materials

- Level 6 Interactive Whiteboard File (level6.notebook)
- *Guess It!* activity sheet (p. 103)
- ballpoint pens or markers

Procedure

1. Launch the Level 6 Notebook file by double-clicking on the icon from the Teacher Resource CD. Press the arrow next to Review activities. Begin this activity by pressing on the Guess It! title from the list.

2. Tell the class that they are going to do an activity to help them review their studies of ancient civilizations. The students should already have an understanding of world history leading up to and including the Roman Empire.

3. Press the arrow to **advance** to the first activity page on the interactive whiteboard and distribute copies of the *Guess It!* activity sheet (p. 103) to students. Also distribute a ballpoint pen or marker to each student.

4. Slide the **screen shade** down until it reveals the first clue to the class (*I was a ruler in the ancient world*). Read the clue aloud. Tell students that the clues will help them guess the identity of the mystery ruler. Have students make a guess and then write it down on their activity sheets next to number "1."

Interactive Whiteboard Skills

- Advancing pages
- Using the screen shade

5. Once all students have written down their guesses, select some of the students to share their guesses to the class. (Students use pens so that they cannot erase and change their guesses.) Now slide the **screen shade** down until the second clue is revealed to the class (*I traveled a great deal*).

6. Select a student to read both clues to the class. Instruct students to record another guess—this time next to number "2." If a student does not want to change his or her guess, have the student write the same name on his or her paper next to number "2."

7. Repeat step 6 until all of the clues are revealed.

8. Slide the **screen shade** all the way to the bottom of the page to reveal the large green rectangle. Ask students how many times they changed their guesses and why they may have changed their guesses.

Review Activities

Guess It! *(cont.)*

Procedure *(cont.)*

9. Press the rectangle to reveal the correct ruler (*I am Julius Caesar*).

10. Press the arrow to **advance** to the next page. Repeat the review game using steps 4–9.

Possible Lesson Ideas

The following lesson suggestions can accompany this review activity:

- Have students each select their own ancient ruler and have them find seven facts about that person. Then have students each create their own Guess It! game using those seven facts. Remind students to place their clues in order from very broad to very specific.

- Have each student take on the role of a particular ancient leader. Have him or her take a notebook page and move around the room interacting with one another, trying to figure out who is acting out which person by asking only yes or no questions. See who can answer the most correctly in the time allotted.

Interactive Whiteboard File

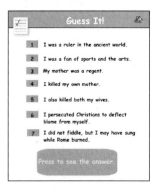

Guess It!

Directions: Read the clues displayed on the board. Record your guesses below.

1. _____

2. _____

3. _____

4. _____

5. _____

6. _____

7. _____

Who am I? _____

1. _____

2. _____

3. _____

4. _____

5. _____

6. _____

7. _____

Who am I? _____

Review Activities

Question It!

Materials

- Level 6 Interactive Whiteboard File (level6.notebook)
- *Question It! Recording Sheet* (p. 106)

Interactive Whiteboard Skills

- Advancing pages
- Dragging objects or text

Procedure

1. Launch the Level 6 Notebook file by double-clicking on the icon from the Teacher Resource CD. Press the arrow next to Review activities. Begin this activity by pressing on the Question It! title from the list.

2. Tell the class that they are going to do an activity to help them review the math skills that they have been studying. Students should already have an understanding of multi-digit multiplication and division, multiplication of fractions, square root, probability, perimeter and area of geometric shapes, and reading points on a graph.

3. Press the arrow to **advance** to the first activity page on the interactive whiteboard and distribute copies of the *Question It! Recording Sheet* (p. 106) to students.

4. Invite a student up to the interactive whiteboard to select a category and a value. Tell students that the easier questions have the lower values and the higher-valued questions are more difficult.

5. Have the student select a question by pushing on a number (e.g., *200*). The question will appear. Although only one student can select a question, instruct every student to copy and solve the question at the bottom of his or her activity sheet. Have students write the letter of the correct answer in the corresponding cell of the question grid on the Recording Sheet.

6. Allow students time to answer the question. Then reveal the answer by **dragging** the yellow box located in the bottom right hand corner to the red X located in the bottom left hand corner. The correct answer will be circled so all students can check their work. Discuss the answer with the class.

7. If the student has the correct answer, have him or her circle the value of the question on his or her answer sheet. For example, the students who answered correctly would circle the 200 on the answer sheet in the "Number Sense" column. If the student has the incorrect answer, have the student place a line through the value of the question.

Review Activities

Question It! *(cont.)*

Procedure *(cont.)*

8. Press the Question It! home button located in the upper right hand corner of the page. This will take the class back to the Question It! home page. Before selecting another student to come up to the interactive whiteboard to choose a new question, **drag** the red X, which is infinitely cloned, over the question that was just selected so that question is not selected again.

9. After the game, have students total their points by adding up all of the numbers that they have circled on their answer sheets. ***Note:*** There are two "Daily Double" questions in this game. If a student selects a question and the "Daily Double" slide appears, it will double the value of the question. For example, if a student selects a question worth 400, it will be doubled to 800.

Possible Lesson Ideas

The following lesson suggestions can accompany this review activity:

- Have the students create their own review questions on 3″x 5″ cards. Partner the students or place them in small groups. Have students mix up the cards and turn them over. One student turns a card over and the first student who says the correct answer gets to keep the card. Students try to collect the most cards.

- Place students into small groups and number each student in the group. Place a question on the interactive whiteboard and have each group work together to solve the problem. Have groups record their answers on small dry-erase boards. After the groups have finished, select a number and have the students who are assigned that number hold up their boards to reveal their answers. Each group with the correct answer gets a point.

Interactive Whiteboard File

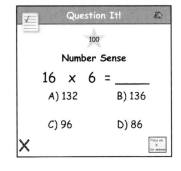

Question It! Recording Sheet

Directions: Use the blank space below to copy and solve the questions that appear on the board. Write the letter of your answer in the corresponding box above. If your answer is correct, circle the number value in the box. If your answer is incorrect, draw a line through the number value in the box.

Number Sense	Probability	Measurement and Geometry
_____ 100	_____ 100	_____ 100
_____ 200	_____ 200	_____ 200
_____ 300	_____ 300	_____ 300
_____ 400	_____ 400	_____ 400
_____ 500	_____ 500	_____ 500

Draw and Guess

Materials

- Level 6 Interactive Whiteboard File (level6.notebook)
- *Draw and Guess Recording Sheet* (p. 109)
- timer

Interactive Whiteboard Skills

- Advancing pages
- Dragging objects or text
- Using the eraser tool
- Using the pen tool

Procedure

1. Launch the Level 6 Notebook file by double-clicking on the icon from the Teacher Resource CD. Press the arrow next to Review activities. Begin this activity by pressing on the Draw and Guess title from the list.

2. Tell the class that they are going to do an activity to help them review some basic parts of speech. They will review nouns, verbs, adjectives, pronouns, prepositions, and adverbs.

3. Place students into five groups around the room. Distribute copies of the *Draw and Guess Recording Sheet* (p. 109) to students. Press the arrow to **advance** to the first activity page on the interactive whiteboard.

4. Invite one student up to the interactive whiteboard from each group. Have each student press the die. The order of play is determined by whoever rolls the highest number. Instruct the remaining students to return to their groups' areas.

5. Assign a game piece to each group. Have the student press the die and move the game piece marked "1" to the appropriate location on the board.

6. Have the student read which part of speech his or her game piece landed on and then press the arrow to **advance** to the next page.

7. If necessary, **drag** the corresponding pull tab from the side of the page to remind students of the definitions of the part of speech that has been selected. Have the student whisper something to draw that is in the category that he or she landed on. For example, if the group landed on "Noun," the student may choose to draw a dog.

8. Tell the student that he or she has one minute to use the **pen tool** to try to draw the thing that he or she chose. Remind the student not to write any letters, numbers, or symbols on the interactive whiteboard—only images—and that colored pens may be used, if desired.

9. Set a timer for one minute. Instruct the student to begin as soon as you start the timer. As the student is drawing the image, allow the other students in the group to call out their guesses.

Review Activities

Draw and Guess *(cont.)*

Procedure *(cont.)*

10. If no one in the group guesses what the image is within one minute, then the group will keep its game piece where it is. Have the student share what he or she was drawing. Instruct everyone in the class to write a sentence using the word that the student was trying to draw on their recording sheets. Use the **eraser tool** to delete the drawing before moving on to the next drawing.

11. If someone in the group guesses correctly, allow the group to go again. The class must still write a sentence using the word before the group can roll the die again. The first group to get its game piece to the "Finish" wins the game.

Possible Lesson Ideas

The following lesson suggestions can accompany this review activity:

- Adapt the game by putting limits on the parts of speech based off of what you have recently been studying. For instance, if you are studying Ancient China in history, require that the words that the students choose have something to do with Ancient China. Or, if you have been studying irregular plural nouns, require that the students use those when they land on the noun box.

- Have students create their own games. Delete all the parts of speech terms on page one and then print it out for each student. Have students place their own terms on the game board and come up with their own rules. Have students work on writing up the rules and procedures for their game.

Interactive Whiteboard File

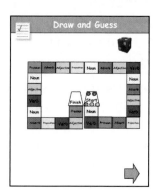

Draw and Guess Recording Sheet

Directions: Write a sentence using the word that was drawn.

1. _____

2. _____

3. _____

4. _____

5. _____

6. _____

7. _____

8. _____

9. _____

10. _____

11. _____

12. _____

13. _____

14. _____

15. _____

16. _____

17. _____

18. _____

19. _____

20. _____

Review Activities

Appendices

References Cited

Becker, C. and M. Lee. 2009. *The interactive whiteboard revolution: Teaching with IWBs.* Victoria, Australia: ACER Press.

Beeland Jr., D. 2002. *Student engagement, visual learning and technology: Can interactive whiteboards help?* Available: http://www.teach.valdosta.edu/are/Artmanscript/vol1no1/beeland_am.pdf

Magaña, S. and P. Frenkel. 2009. *Transforming teaching and learning for the 21st century.* Available: http://www.prometheanworld.com/upload/pdf/transforming_Teaching_and_Learning_for_the_21st _Century_V6.pdf

Marzano, R. J. 2009. *The art and science of teaching: Teaching with interactive whiteboards.* Educational Leadership 67 (November): 80–82.

Marzano, R. J., and M. Haystead. 2009. *Final report on the evaluation of the Promethean technology.* Englewood, CO: Marzano Research Laboratory.

Torff, B. and R. Tirotta, 2010. Interactive whiteboards produce small gains in elementary students' self-reported motivation in mathematics. *Computers & Education* 54: 370–383.

Literature cited

Rawls, Wilson. *Where the Red Fern Grows.* New York: Doubleday, 1961.

Answer Key

Word Mix-up (p. 22)
1. vegetables, fruits, grains; Healthy Foods
2. heart rate, breathing rate, intensity; Exercise Monitoring

Analogies Matter (p. 25)
1. atom is to matter as brick is to wall
2. corrosion is to rust as burning is to ash
3. H_2O is to water as NaCL is to table salt
4. solid is to liquid as liquid is to gas

Today's Snapshot (p. 28)
Responses will vary.

Daily Geography (p. 31)
1. Vergina
2. Peloponnesos
3. The Aegean Sea
4. Sparta
5. B
6. C
7. B
8. A

Math Practice (p. 34)
1. 13,878
2. 7
3. $n = 298$
4. 14,257
5. $271.6\bar{6}$
6. 12 in.
7. 142,657.11
8. 70
9. 19

Drawing Comparisons (p. 37)
1. Responses will vary.
2. Responses will vary.
3. Responses will vary.

Answer Key *(cont.)*

Concept of Definition Map (p. 40)

Responses depend on class discussion.

Example/Nonexample (p. 43)

whole number: Examples—14; 8,123,456; 1; 0 Nonexamples—π; -14; $\frac{1}{4}$; $\sqrt{14}$; .14; .256; $-\frac{1}{2}$

integer: Examples—14; 8,123,456; 1; 0; -14 Nonexamples—π; $\frac{1}{4}$; $\sqrt{14}$; .14; .256; $-\frac{1}{2}$

rational number: Examples—14; 8,123,456; 1; 0; -14; $\frac{1}{4}$; $\sqrt{14}$; .14; .256; $-\frac{1}{2}$

Nonexamples—π

Dynasty Actions (p. 46)

Dynasty	Rulers of Note	Characteristics	Time Period	Student/Action
Xia Dynasty	Yu	flood control, jade work, bronze weapons, human sacrifice	2200 BCE–1760 BCE	Action will depend on class discussion.
Shang Dynasty	Di Xin	walled cities, bronze metalwork, rulers had large tombs, oracle bones, writing	1760 BCE–1046 BCE	Action will depend on class discussion.
Zhou Dynasty (Western and Eastern)	Wen	mandate of Heaven, expansion, warlords, cavalry	1046 BCE–481 BCE	Action will depend on class discussion.
Qin Dynasty	Shi Huangdi	Great Wall, unification, First Emperor, central government and code of laws, standardization, censorship	221 BCE–210 BCE	Action will depend on class discussion.
Han Dynasty	Liu Bang and Wudi	Confucian principles of government, peace, trade routes, farming, ironwork, arts flourished, paper invented	206 BCE–220 CE (interrupted briefly by Xin 9–23 CE)	Action will depend on class discussion.

When Is a Verb Not a Verb? (p. 49)

gerund: meaning—ends in "ing," verb used as a noun; Possible words—*appearing, approving, climbing, cooking, judging, playing, spelling, traveling, watching,* and *working*

infinitive: meaning—starts with "to." Verb can be used as a noun, adjective, or adverb; Possible words—*to appear, to approve, to climb, to cook, to judge, to learn, to match, to play, to spell, to travel, to watch*

participle: meaning—ends in "ing" or "ed," verb used as an adjective; Possible words—*appeared, approved, climbed, cooked, judged, learned, matched, played, spelled, traveled, watched, worked*

1. traveling
2. watched
3. frowning
4. to laugh

Answer Key *(cont.)*

Picture Analysis (p. 52)

Responses will vary.

Anticipation Guide (p. 55)

Responses will vary.

Famous Speech (p. 58)

Responses will vary.

Vertebrates (p. 61)

Responses will vary.

Mathematical Relations (p. 64)

rotation; dilation

Comparing Societies (p. 67)

Responses will vary.

Order of Operations (p. 70)

1. Think PEMDAS
2. $7 \times 3 + (-2)^2$
3. $7 \times 3 + 4$
4. $21 + 4$
5. 25
6. Remember to check your work!

1. Think PEMDAS
2. Parentheses: Work from the inside out.
3. Exponents: Work these next.
4. Multiplication and Division: Work from left to right.
5. Addition and Subtraction: Work from left to right.
6. Remember to check your work!

My KWL (p. 73)

Responses will vary.

Verb Agreement (p. 76)

Verb	Subject	Verb Form That Agrees with the Subject
to run	Stephanie and Martha	run
to grow	Jason	grows
to be	the turtles	are
to begin	several summers	begin
to have	five of my favorite people	have
to survive	Yosemite	survives
to learn	a student	learns

Sentences will vary.

Answer Key *(cont.)*

Eukaryote Web (p. 79)

protists; fungi; plants; animals

Responses will vary.

Causes and Effects (p. 82)

Cause: Layers of sediment build up over millions of years.

Possible Effect: Sedimentary rock forms.

Cause: Hot liquid magma flows into cool water.

Possible Effect: The magma cools into igneous rock.

Cause: Igneous or sedimentary rock is put under great heat and pressure.

Possible Effect: It becomes metamorphic rock.

What to Do with Shapes (p. 85)

Shapes with Equal Sides	Shapes with Unequal Sides	Shapes with Curves

Monochromatic Ink Brush Painting (p. 88)

Main Idea: Monochromatic ink brush painting is a traditional Asian art form.

Details: Responses will vary.

Answer Key *(cont.)*

Flashing Back into Sequence (p. 91)

First, Gerald takes medicine.

Second, Gerald remembers healthier times.

Third, Ellie wins at tennis.

Fourth, Ellie challenges Gerald to a race.

Fifth, Gerald decides to get healthy.

Finally, Gerald challenges Ellie to a race.

Story Summary (p. 94)

Responses will vary.

Linking matter (p. 97)

Responses will vary.

Review Game (p. 100)

Responses will vary.

Guess It! (p. 103)

1. I am Julius Caesar.
2. I am Nero.

Question It! (p. 106)

	Number Sense	Probability	Measurement and Geometry
100	C	C	A
200	B	B	C
300	A	B	D
400	D	A	B
500	C	C	D

Draw and Guess (p. 109)

Responses will vary.

Content-Area Matrix

Content Area	Activity Title
Mathematics	• Daily Mathematics • Example/Nonexample • Picture Predictions • Flow Chart • Classify and Categorize • Question It!
Science	• Analogies • Alike and Different • List, Group, Label • Web Map • Cause and Effect • Content Links
Social Studies	• Daily Geography • Total Physical Response • Analyze the Picture • Venn Diagram • Main Idea and Details • Guess It!
Reading	• Anagram Words • Concept of Definition Map • Anticipation Guide • T-Chart • Sequencing • Game Board
Writing	• Calendar • Word Tiles • Historical Document • KWL Chart • Summarizing • Draw and Guess

How-to Guide

Advancing pages

1. When in slideshow view on the interactive whiteboard, press the forward arrow from the toolbar.

2. In full screen view, press the forward arrow on the floating toolbar.

3. If you want to move to the previous page, press the backward arrow.

4. To return to the home menu page, press the house icon on the top of the page.

1.    **2.**   **4.**

Saving a file

1. When viewing a file on a computer, select **File** from the menu across the top of the page.

2. Then select *Save*.

3. When viewing the file on an interactive whiteboard, select the cursor tool from the toolbar.

4. Then press the *Save* icon on the toolbar.

2. 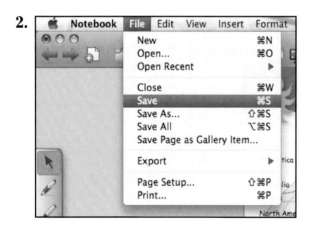   **3.**    **4.**

How-to Guide *(cont.)*

Dragging objects or text

1. Select the cursor tool from the toolbar.

2. Press on the desired object or piece of text.

3. Without lifting your finger, drag the object or text to the desired location.

1.  **3.**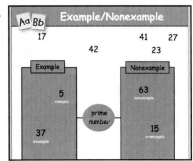

Using the eraser

1. Select the eraser tool from the toolbar.

2. Choose the width of the eraser by pressing the desired box with your finger.

3. Pick up the eraser tool from the shelf on the interactive whiteboard. Use it like a regular eraser to delete the desired text or drawings. ***Note:*** The eraser will only remove information recorded with the pen tool.

1.  **3.**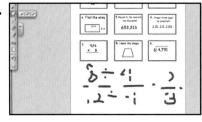

Using the highlighting tool

1. Select the pen tool from the toolbar.

2. Select either the yellow highlighter or the green highlighter from the menu by pressing the desired box with your finger.

3. Highlight desired text by dragging the pen over the text.

3.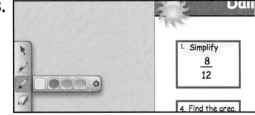

How-to Guide *(cont.)*

Using the pen tool

1. Select the pen tool from the toolbar.

2. Select a color or style from the menu by pressing the desired box with your finger.

3. Write or draw using the pen.

3.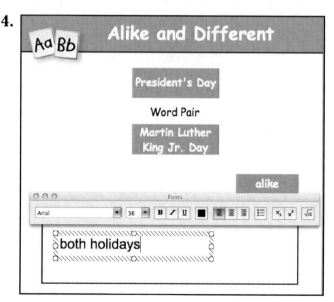

Using the text tool

1. Select the text tool from the toolbar.

2. Select the desired text size.

3. Press anywhere on the screen that you would like text to appear.

4. Type the desired text.

5. Select the cursor tool and grab the text to move it around the page, if desired.

2. 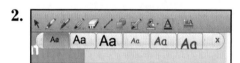   **4.**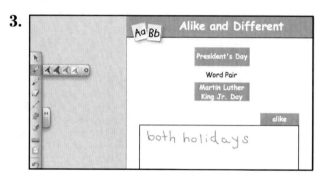

How-to Guide *(cont.)*

Using dual page display

1. Select the dual page display icon from the toolbar. The screen will divide in half and the current page will be displayed on the right.

2. Press the arrow to advance the current page to the left. The next page will appear on the right. The two pages can now be viewed and manipulated side-by-side.

1.

Pinning pages

1. Select the dual page display icon from the toolbar. The screen will divide in half and the current page will be displayed on the right.

2. Press the arrow to advance the page you want to be pinned until it appears on the right side of the display.

3. Select the pin page tool from the toolbar. This will pin the current page displayed on the left.

4. If you do not have the pin page tool on your toolbar, use the computer to select **View** from the main toolbar menu, then select ***Zoom*** from the drop-down menu.

5. Then select *pin page* from the second drop-down menu. This will pin the current page displayed on the left.

1.

3.

5.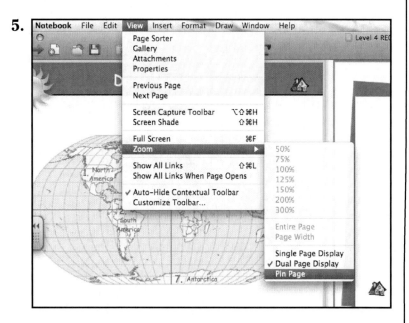

How-to Guide *(cont.)*

Using the cell shade

Note: The cell shade only works when using a table.

1. When viewing a table file on a computer, right click in the cell into which you want to insert the cell shade.

2. Select ***Add Cell Shade*** from the drop-down menu. The cell shade appears.

3. To remove the cell shade, select the cursor tool from the toolbar then press the cell shade with your finger.

4. When viewing a file on the interactive whiteboard, use the mouse buttons on the front of the interactive whiteboard to right click in the cell into which you want to insert the cell shade. Then repeat steps 2 and 3 above.

2. 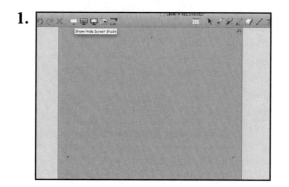   **3.**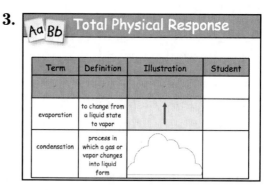

Using the screen shade

1. Select the show/hide screen shade tool from the toolbar. A screen shade will appear on the entire screen.

2. Adjust the size of the screen shade by dragging the top or sides of the shade.

3. To reveal the hidden information, drag the desired portion of the screen shade slowly.

4. To remove the shade completely, press the red circle in the top right corner of the shade.

1. 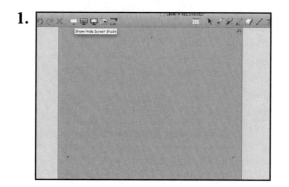   **2.**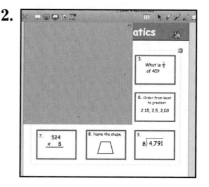

How-to Guide *(cont.)*

Using the spotlight tool

1. Select the spotlight tool from the toolbar. To turn on the spotlight tool, select the customize floating tools icon located at the bottom of the vertical tool bar. Then select **Other Interactive Whiteboard Tools** and then *Spotlight* from the drop-down menu. The screen will go dark except for a single circle.

2. To change the size or location of the circle, grab and drag the spotlight using any black portion of the screen.

3. To change the shape of the spotlight, select *Shape* from the drop-down menu on the spotlight shown on the screen. Choose the desired shape from the second dropdown menu that appears.

4. To change the transparency of the background, select *Transparency* from the drop-down menu on the spotlight shown on the screen. Choose the desired transparency from the second drop-down menu that appears.

4.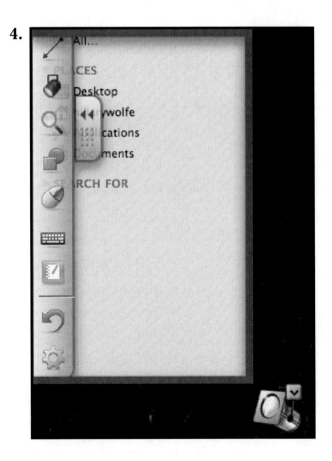

Interactive Whiteboard Skills Matrix

Activity Title	Interactive Whiteboard Skills Used
Anagrams	• Advancing pages • Dragging objects or text • Using the screen shade • Using the spotlight tool
Analogies	• Advancing pages • Dragging objects or text
Calendar	• Advancing pages • Dragging objects or text • Using the pen tool
Daily Geography	• Advancing pages • Dragging objects or text • Pinning pages • Using dual page display
Daily Math	• Advancing pages • Dragging objects or text • Using the spotlight tool
Alike and Different	• Advancing pages • Using dual page display • Using the pen tool • Using the text tool
Concept of Definition Map	• Advancing pages • Using the pen tool • Using the text tool
Example/Nonexample	• Advancing pages • Dragging objects or text • Using the pen tool • Using the text tool
Total Physical Response	• Advancing pages • Using the cell shade • Using the pen tool • Using the text tool

Interactive Whiteboard Skills Matrix *(cont.)*

Activity Title	Interactive Whiteboard Skills Used
Word Tiles	• Advancing pages • Dragging objects or text
Analyze the Picture	• Advancing pages • Dragging objects or text
Anticipation Guide	• Advancing pages • Dragging objects or text • Using the pen tool
Historical Document	• Advancing pages • Dragging objects or text • Using the spotlight tool
List, Group, Label	• Advancing pages • Dragging objects or text • Using the pen tool • Using the text tool
Picture Prediction	• Advancing pages • Dragging objects or text • Using the pen tool • Using the text tool
Venn Diagram	• Advancing pages • Dragging objects or text • Using the pen tool • Using the text tool
Flow Chart	• Advancing pages • Dragging objects or text • Using the pen tool • Using the text tool
KWL Chart	• Advancing pages • Using the pen tool • Using the screen shade • Using the text tool
T-Chart	• Advancing pages • Dragging objects or text • Using the pen tool

Interactive Whiteboard Skills Matrix *(cont.)*

Activity Title	Interactive Whiteboard Skills Used
Web Map	• Advancing pages • Dragging objects or text • Pinning pages *(optional)* • Using dual page display *(optional)* • Using the pen tool • Using the text tool
Cause and Effect	• Advancing pages • Dragging objects or text
Classify and Categorize	• Advancing pages • Dragging objects or text • Using the eraser • Using the pen tool
Main Idea and Details	• Advancing pages • Using the highlighting tool • Using the pen tool • Using the text tool
Sequencing	• Advancing pages • Dragging objects or text • Using dual page display • Using the highlighting tool • Using the pen tool • Using the text tool
Summarizing	• Using the pen tool • Using the spotlight tool • Using the text tool
Content Links	• Advancing pages • Dragging objects or text • Using the pen tool
Game Board	• Advancing pages • Dragging objects or text
Guess It!	• Advancing pages • Using the screen shade
Question It!	• Advancing pages • Dragging objects or text
Draw and Guess	• Advancing pages • Dragging objects or text • Using the eraser tool • Using the pen tool

Contents of the Teacher Resource CD

Teacher Resources

Activity	File Name
Interactive Whiteboard files	Level6.notebook
Instructional Time Line	timeline.pdf
How-to Guide	how-to.pdf

Student Reproducibles

Activity	File Name
Getting Started Activities	
Word Mix-up	page22.pdf
Analogies Matter	page25.pdf
Today's Snapshot	page28.pdf
Daily Geography	page31.pdf
Math Practice	page34.pdf
Vocabulary Development Activities	
Drawing Comparisons	page37.pdf
Concept of Definition Map	page40.pdf
Example/Nonexample	page43.pdf
Dynasty Actions	page46.pdf
When Is a Verb Not a Verb?	page49.pdf
Activating Prior Knowledge Activities	
Picture Analysis	page52.pdf
Anticipation Guide	page55.pdf
Famous Speech	page58.pdf
Vertebrates	page61.pdf
Mathematical Relations	page64.pdf
Graphic Organizer Activities	
Comparing Societies	page67.pdf
Order of Operations	page70.pdf
My KWL	page73.pdf
Verb Agreement	page76.pdf
Eukaryote Web	page79.pdf
Comprehension Activities	
Causes and Effects	page82.pdf
What To Do with Shapes	page85.pdf
Monochromatic Ink Brush Painting	page88.pdf
Flashing Back into Sequence	page91.pdf
Story Summary	page94.pdf
Review Activities	
Linking Matter	page97.pdf
Review Game	page100.pdf
Guess It!	page103.pdf
Question It! Recording Sheet	page106.pdf
Draw and Guess Recording Sheet	page109.pdf

Notes